Marijuana
Outdoor Grower's Guide
The Secrets to Growing a Natural Marijuana Garden

S. T. Oner

T0038500

Marijuana
Outdoor Grower's Guide
The Secrets to Growing a Natural Marijuana Garden

S. T. Oner

Green Candy Press

Marijuana Outdoor Grower's Guide
The Secrets to Growing a Natural Marijuana Garden
Published by Green Candy Press

Copyright © 2010 S.T. Oner

ISBN 978-1937866-90-7
eBook ISBN 978-1-937866-91-4

1st edition ISBN 978-1-931160-41-4

Copyright © 2007 S.T. Oner

Cover photo © David Strange

Photographs © Andre Grossman, Autofem Seeds, CH9 Feminized Seeds, Delta 9 Labs, Dr. Greenthumb Seeds, D. Strange, Dutch Passion Seeds, Ed Borg, Green Devil Genetics Seed Company, Greenhouse Seed Co., LF Images, KC Brains Seeds, MG Imaging, Paradise Seeds, Pepper Design, Sagarmatha Seeds, Sativa Steph, Sensi Seeds, and Soma Seeds.

This book contains information about illegal substances, specifically the plant Cannabis Sativa and its derivative products. Green Candy Press would like to emphasize that Cannabis is a controlled substance in North America and throughout much of the world. As such, the use and cultivation of cannabis can carry heavy penalties that may threaten an individual's liberty and livelihood.

The aim of the Publisher is to educate and entertain. Whatever the Publisher's view on the validity of current legislation, we do not in any way condone the use of prohibited substances.

All rights reserved. No part of this book may be reproduced in any form without express written permission from the Publisher, except by a reviewer, who may quote brief passages or reproduce illustrations in a review where appropriate credit is given. Nor may any part of this book be reproduced, stored in a retrieval system, or transmitted in any form or by any means without written permission from the Publisher.

Printed in China by 1010 Printing.
Sometimes Massively Distributed by P.G.W.

Acknowledgements

I would like to dedicate this book, as I have with all of my other books, to NORML and everyone who has fought against the war on drug users. In addition, I would like to thank the incredible people and organizations that contributed to this, the second edition of the *Marijuana Outdoor Grower's Guide*.

I'd like to thank Andre Grossman, Autofem Seeds, CH9 Feminized Seeds, Delta 9 Labs, Dr. Greenthumb Seeds, D. Strange, Dutch Passion Seeds, Ed Borg, Green Devil Genetics Seed Company, Greenhouse Seed Co., LF Images, KC Brains Seeds, MG Imaging, Paradise Seeds, Pepper Design, Sagarmatha Seeds, Sativa Steph, Sensi Seeds, and Soma Seeds for their support and help with this project.

There are some contributors who wish to remain anonymous for various reasons, but who deserve recognition and respect nonetheless, and everyone on the online forums who helped me out, as well, especially the people at Breedbay. co.uk and 420magazine.com.

I would also like to thank my family for their unwavering support and to Cannabis Sativa, for her continuous supply of outdoor growing challenges.

I would also like to thank the growers, breeders and writers who inspired me to learn more about this incredible plant; Ed Rosenthal, Greg Green, Mel Frank, and Jorge Cervantes are some big ones, and of course Jack Herer, may he rest in peace. You guys are incredible, and I wouldn't be able to do what I do without the work you have accomplished.

— *S. T. Oner*

Contents

Decriminalization: Hopeful Shoots

History records the use of marijuana since ancient times. This incredibly versatile plant has been used by societies the world over—as a durable fabric, strong fiber, fuel, and medicine, as well as for its unique recreational (and gastronomic!) properties. Yet possession and cultivation of marijuana is considered criminal in many countries today.

This is the result of global prohibition efforts initiated in the last century whose effects have been enormous in both cost and scope, while doing little to decrease actual drug consumption and traffic. To take the United States as an example, overall drug use has increased since the US "War on Drugs" of the 1980s.

One thing that the War on Drugs has achieved is the incarceration of large numbers of nonviolent offenders. This has had a chilling effect on marijuana users. In 2001, more than 700,000 marijuana-related arrests were made in the United States alone. According to NORML (the National Organization for the Reform of Marijuana Laws), almost six million Americans have been arrested since 1992. This is a "greater number than the entire populations of Alaska, Delaware, the District of Columbia, Montana, North Dakota, South Dakota, Vermont and Wyoming combined." What all of this makes abundantly clear is that prohibitionist governments are actively fighting a war, but not against drugs: the aggression is aimed at their own citizens.

There are signs of a trend towards legalization, most notably in states like California, Colorado and Oregon where the citizens have passed ballot initiatives that have legalized the medicinal use of marijuana. Internationally, Spain, England and, of course the Netherlands are among those countries to have taken the most progressive steps forward. Yet even in states and countries with more liberal drug policies certain unfair restrictions are placed on both growers and consumers.

Informed is Empowered

The best advice that I can offer prospective marijuana growers is to exercise caution and, above all, to be aware of precisely what is and is not permissible under the law. It is also important to be aware of the severity of any potential penalties before you commit to growing marijuana. In some countries, the laws, their enforcement, and the penalties for breaking them vary regionally. In the United States, laws may vary from state to state and the penalties can vary dramatically depending on the quantity of marijuana and paraphernalia involved.

Information about marijuana laws in many countries is relatively easily accessed through a variety of publicly available resources. Perhaps the best research tool is the Internet. Federal and local governments, as well as international policy associations like NORML (www.norml.org) offer much of this information online.

Common sense is usually your best defense, and can go a long way toward keeping you out of harm's way. Avoid dealing or transporting marijuana whenever possible, and pay special attention to pipes and other paraphenalia that can be left accidentally in open view of others. This is especially important to the outdoor cultivator during the long growing season, because you will be making frequent trips to your growing site. Do not speed, drive recklessly or otherwise attract unwanted attention, since a simple visual search can invite a lot of uncomfortable questioning by the authorities. During each excursion to your growing site, take the necessary precautions. The best advice is not to tell anyone that you are growing.

Though this book will outline the steps necessary for successful cultivation of marijuana, it is not an endorsement or invitation to break the law. The information provided here is simply that: information.

Cultivating: A Passion

Many people who grow plants of any kind have found the experience edifying, in that the act of caring for their plants connects them to their environment. Plants react instantly to subtle changes in light, soil, and temperature that might otherwise go unnoticed. Being at an outdoor growing site in the natural environment can be a relaxing counterbalance to the world of steel, concrete, and microprocessors that surrounds us every day.

Selecting the best females and performing involved tasks like cloning and pruning seem to help people

Preface

connect to individual plants in ways that don't happen with the ficus in one's living room. Since there are many steps to be performed, and a lot of things to keep in mind, many people enjoy the challenge of growing plants—marijuana or otherwise.

For me, growing plants successfully can be compared to the satisfaction of creating a special meal. In fact, using herbs that you have grown yourself in your cuisine actually does make the food taste better! You can expect the first joint or batch of brownies made from your very first harvest, grown from scratch, to be an extremely memorable and rewarding experience. It truly has become my passion.

A Word About Marijuana Use

As a chef, I naturally have a passion for all things culinary and tend to use my grow to enhance my cooking. That said, I recognize that pot is consumed in many different ways: it can be vaporized, smoked, ingested, drank and more. In this book, I will use these terms interchangeably to describe marijuana consumption. Personally, I believe that eating is the best and most efficient way to enjoy pot, however smoking is probably the most common method. If you are going to smoke your grow, I strongly recommend vaporizers as they limit your intake of the tar, carbon monoxide and other nonpsychoactive substances that occur upon burning marijuana. I have also included a pot butter recipe at the end of this book in the hope that this might persuade budding marijuana chefs to make the switch from smoking to cooking with marijuana. At the very least, it is an excellent way to stretch your harvest.

Whatever your motivation to start growing, and however you use your grow, I hope that you will find this book to be a good companion along the road to the first of many bountiful outdoor harvests!

But, always remember the most important thing is to be aware of your local laws.

Help Sow The Seeds of Reform

JOIN NORML TODAY

National organization for

the reform of marijuana laws

www.norml.org

Growing Your Own Marijuana Outdoors

Marijuana is a very versatile plant that can, and does, grow well untended in a wide variety of geographic areas. This is obviously to the grower's advantage since increased pressure from law enforcement has forced many people to seek sites that are in remote locations.

Benefits for the Grower

In the 1960s it was common to plant marijuana on the hills around your house, or, interspersed with other plants in your backyard, but the War on Drugs and the increased hysteria surrounding drug use have made this option untenable. The best sites, therefore, are southern-facing slopes on hillsides on public property. This limits your liability since, should the worst happen, the plants are less likely to be traced back to you. As long as you have access to your site during the critical early months, and it has an adequate water supply, you can leave the plants there and return to find that they have grown into monster bud-factories.

Better Quality Pot, Naturally

In my mind, pot grown outdoors is the best in the world for a variety of reasons. First and foremost, outdoor plants are grown in their natural environment. Under the right conditions, all of the nutrients and water required to sustain healthy and vigorous plant growth are provided naturally. Also, when grown outdoors, buds typically grow to a larger size than is possible when cultivation takes place solely indoors, where space is limited. Depending on the nutrients and the amount of water supplied, a mature outdoor marijuana plant can easily reach heights of seven or more feet, sometimes twelve foot and up with the equatorial Sativa variety. Outdoor plants grow to these great heights over the course of a season by generating a tremendous amount of energy from the sheer quantity of their leaves, a process called photosynthesis. As the season ends, this energy is converted to flowering, which helps to create dense, heavy buds. Four or five of these large buds will suffice for a year's supply, depending on how much you want to consume, and can be harvested from one to two plants. By comparison, indoor plants are typically smaller, which means their buds are also smaller, so more plants must be cultivated inside in order to achieve the same bud amounts as a single outdoor plant.

Reduced Security Risk

There are many reasons to decide to grow your own marijuana outdoors. One of these must certainly be security. I have a friend who grows on the third floor of his apartment building. As you clear the second landing, you start to

Producing your own bud is a sweet reward.

pick up faint traces of weed. Walking down the hallway to his door, the smell is very powerful, especially if the door has been opened recently. A lot of space in his apartment is devoted to the effort. He has closets for his seedlings, and two separate closets for the older plants as they move into maturity and flowering. Besides the lights, heat, and smell, growing inside can increase the risks—the plants are always in your home or on your property and can be traced back to you. Unless you severely limit the number of people who are allowed in, the fact that you are growing will be evident to at least a few individuals. One way of reducing indoor odor problems is by using an activated carbon filter.

Bigger Yields

Though my indoor grower friend has a year-round harvest, if he were able to grow outdoors he would abandon his indoor setup immediately, for largely one reason: the yields. When grown indoors, the plants can never grow very large. Using half as much energy and time he could produce plants two to three times larger with bigger buds. Instead of cutting his plants for a few pounds, he could reap an annual harvest in October of 12 to 15 pounds—more than enough to last him until next season!

Benefits for the End User

Increased Control

Strong, healthy outdoor plants will produce large yields—enough pot to keep you smiling for months to come—but perhaps an even better benefit is that you are in control of what you consume. When you grow something, you know everything that has happened to the plant, from the nursery to your pipe. The seeds you used, the strain you chose, and the time you invested in caring for the plant, will all be reflected in your high. You can personally attest to its freshness, and you don't have to worry that anyone has tampered with it.

Better Quality Pot and No Adulterates

Walking in most major cities, you will receive offers of weed for purchase, but those bags are often light, or maybe they've been fluffed with a generous helping of seeds and stems. It is not uncommon to notice that some of the weed has been picked and dried in such a way that the color has changed from complex greens and purples, to a dull brown that smokes harshly, and is as likely to give you a headache as produce a high. The experience can leave you wondering why you've decided to even smoke pot.

In general, smoking pot, or for that matter smoking almost anything, is not harmless. Though much has been made of the amount of cancer-causing agents in marijuana as compared to cigarettes; it wouldn't be unreasonable to assume that a lot of this has been somewhat overstated in the media and understated by marijuana advocacy groups. In a general way, smoking marijuana is far less dangerous for your health than smoking cigarettes, mainly due to the way in which it is smoked. A famous (and often misquoted) study was released by Dr. Tashkin, which equated 1 joint to 16 cigarettes. Dr. Tashkin himself has

This fence is to provide protection from small predators.

refuted the study largely because of the way the information has been used. The quote below, excerpted from NORML's web site, helps to explains Dr. Tashkin's frustration.

A more widely accepted estimate is that marijuana smokers consume four times as much carcinogenic tar as cigarettes smokers per weight smoked. This does not necessarily mean that one joint equals four cigarettes, since joints usually weigh less. In fact, the average joint has been estimated to contain 0.4 grams of pot, a bit less than one-half the weight of a cigarette, making one joint equal to two cigarettes (actually, joint sizes range from cigar-sized spliffs smoked by Rastas, to very fine sinsemilla joints weighing as little as 0.2 grams). It should be noted that there is no exact

This Jack 33 plant from CH9 Female Seeds is known to be very straightforward to grow indoors and outdoors and offers an energetic, uplifting high.

equivalency between tobacco and marijuana smoking, because they affect different parts of the respiratory tract differently: whereas tobacco tends to penetrate to the smaller, peripheral passageways of the lungs, pot tends to concentrate on the larger, central passageways. One consequence of this is that pot, unlike tobacco, does not appear to cause emphysema.*

Great tight bud that is going to be a nice smoke.

Less Hassle

Having control over what you smoke (and the price) is good not only because you will save money and increase control, but also because you won't have to worry about being given low quality buds at a high price, and being forced to wait for it. While your friends are calling and waiting for someone to magically appear with some green, you can simply reach into your freezer and select exactly which strain and how much you want to smoke.

Nice compact bud.

Reduced Risk

There is always a risk on the street, or even with a dealer that you know. In many states where draconian drug laws are on the books, buying pot can be a decision that could impact the next three to ten years of your life. The risk of being ensnared in this dragnet is greatly increased when you transact with known dealers, rather than when your pot supplier is your freezer.

Loose schwag.

Chapter 1

This Annunaki from DNA Genetics is 75% Sativa and 25% Indica, a beautiful strain for outdoors.

Some Disadvantages

The Pest Problem: Plant Pests, Predators, Police, and Passersby

Growing marijuana outside carries its own risks that are your responsibility to investigate. In the event of a bust, the major piece of evidence that will be used against you is your grow, which is why growing inside presents so many hassles. This is why it is so important to keep the plants off your own land. Many states have seizure laws that afford law enforcement the right to take everything, including things that were not directly used to grow the plants.

One grower in the Santa Cruz area of California has tried to combat this issue by quietly transferring the deed for his house and land to the woman he lives with. Since they are not married, in the event of a raid, only he, and not the land, the house, and so forth could be seized. This solution may work for him, but is not appropriate for everyone, and you have to very careful even when growing on public land. If the police suspect you and have been monitoring your growing site, they may be able to catch you in the act.

The police, with their helicopters, sophisticated monitoring equipment, and network of informants, though certainly no friend to the outdoor grower, are not your biggest problem. Growing outside means being at the mercy of nature. There are many pests and predators, from insects to deer, that view your plants as being yet more vegetable matter that is good to eat. There are certain precautions you can take, but you should be aware that none of them are foolproof.

Placing lion urine or chemical insecticides around your grow can go a long way toward repelling things that fly, crawl, or walk on four legs, but it won't stop the pests that walk on two. On public lands, hunters, hikers, and accidental passersby can all report you to the authorities or take unwanted deductions from your plant. This is why humans are perhaps the worst pests of all. Opportunists can monitor your plant's growth and harvest your babies a day or two before you were planning to, thereby benefiting from all of your hard work. Many growers report that the biggest problem is finding an area that is not near trails, has a water supply, and yet is reasonably accessible and not completely overrun with wildlife.

If you pick an area that is not frequented by people, there is still one other group that is especially dangerous: your friends. Being a grower means being tight-lipped about the source and location of your pot. Friends and ex-girlfriends have been known to do everything from steal, to tip the cops off to the location of growing sites. Keeping quiet may be difficult, especially when the conversation turns

Be very aware of your local laws before you decide to grow.

Security of your grow is an important issue. Predators come in many shapes and sizes.

to the availability of marijuana, or to your views on decriminalization, but in the court of life, anything you say may be used against you.

The Patience and Planning Problem: Learning to Grow and Nurture Your Plants

The other notable drawback to planting outdoors is that it does require some planning and forethought, constant vigilance, and patience. It is important to start at the right time—a few weeks before planting season—and to stay the course for five to eight months depending on the growing season in your part of the world.

As any farmer, or even backyard gardener, can attest, there is more to growing a plant than simply throwing seeds into the ground, adding water, and walking away. The first time you grow, your yield may not be as big as you had envisioned. There is a learning curve, and if this is your first attempt at growing anything—even houseplants—then it may take two or three growing seasons to realize truly high yields. Each year, you will learn one or two more tricks and understand the process better and it will pay off in spades. The early failures, which may be discouraging at first, will be repaid to you later each time you open your freezer and see the enormous amount of pot stored there. Each time you smoke, you'll feel a little satisfaction that you know everything about what you are putting into your body.

Growing plants, even those that are fairly resilient, is not a foolproof process, and there are many points along the way when the crops may be threatened. Moving a plant, as in a transplant, can cause it to undergo shock and even die, but many times throughout your plant's life this may be necessary. There are ways to do this correctly but it can't be rushed and proper attention must be paid. Other potential pitfalls include growing the wrong sex of plant and letting your plants go to seed instead of focusing on flower production.

There are many such pitfalls that this book will help you to avoid. My goal is to set you on the right path—one that leads to a successful growing season and the visual feast that awaits when you see your first real harvest, piled high!

This grow on a back deck is sure to provide a bumper harvest. Bamboo screens help to hide it from neighbors.

Camping right beside your grow is not the best idea.

Chapter 2

Seed and Strain Selection

Good bud, with a nice aroma, flavorful taste, and high potency, starts with good genetics. Even though each seed is a genetic blueprint of an individual plant, there is still a variation within strains. All plants grown from seed will vary slightly in their development unless the strain is considered stable and the growing environment is similar. Growing is an unpredictable science unless you already have knowledge of the plant that your seeds or clones come from. A good idea, in order to ensure better harvests year-to-year is to pick one of your best plants, and seed it (or clone it), thus ensuring this selection will work for you. People who have been growing plants for a few years and continually choosing the strongest plant of that strain will have much better seeds to begin their next crop with.

Start With Good Genetics

Consider the Source and the Destination

Each area of the world in which pot is grown produces seeds and, eventually, marijuana that is distinct to both its climate and the preferences of the grower. Marijuana grown in the tropics tends to have tiny leaves, with an abundance of flowers, while Middle Eastern, and central Asian varieties will usually feature long broad leaves and dense buds. These differences may be important to note. The size of the leaves has a lot to do with the strength and consistency of the sunlight. Larger leaves are essential if your light is weak since they have more surface area with which to trap the sun's rays.

Knowing where a plant has normally been grown may prove beneficial to your own efforts. Growers in Florida, or other humid subtropical areas such as Louisiana, Texas, and along the Gulf Coast, may wish to capitalize on climate by planting tropical types. Some people might prefer to stick to a hardy stock like Mexican, which comes in many varieties and colors, or perhaps Jamaican weed, which is extremely hardy and durable.

It is important to remember that climate and the particular strain can only tell you how well a plant might flourish in your area. For instance, it might not make sense to plant a Hawaiian variety like Maui, if your growing season is shorter than its native habitat, exposing it to less than optimal levels of sunlight or an early frost. Though the plant will produce a smokeable yield that will get you high, even in suboptimal conditions, the size of the plant before harvesting may be small and consequently your yields will

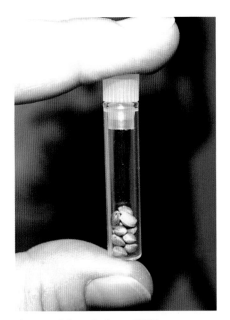

Annunaki seeds from DNA.

CH9 Female Seeds' Super Haze Fem is 70% Sativa and 30% Indica with a spicy, floral taste. She is a tough girl that is perfect for indoor and outdoor growers.

be smaller than desired.

If you've smoked different varieties of pot, you'll notice that the highs can differ greatly. Some highs feel happy or dreamy, whereas others may take a longer time to set in and make you feel sleepy. Then there are the bad highs, or the ones that give you a headache, a sore throat, or make you feel paranoid. This should be your real guiding principle when choosing seeds. This is an issue of chemistry and the best way to replicate the good highs and avoid cultivating the bad highs, is to obtain seeds from the stuff you like and also to cure the bud properly after harvest. This is relatively easy because seeds are, to many growers, the useless by-product of growing. Depending on the methods used by the grower, there could be many seeds left over. There are also online companies that offer seeds with photo galleries that show the potential outcome. As with any online purchase, the responsibility is yours to investigate the legitimacy of the company. Also, knowledge of the law regarding the purchase of possession of seeds in your area is important as it may be illegal to possess them.

A Quick Note on the Chemistry of Marijuana

The active ingredient in marijuana is Delta-9 tetrahydrocannabinol, commonly referred to as THC. This is imprecise because there are other forms of THC that are slightly different from Delta-9, like Delta-8. In addition, there are other active chemicals that contribute to the high. These compounds, known as cannabinoids, include all the variations of THC and are the psychoactive ingredients of the plant—the reason you get "high." Most marijuana contains between 1 and 6% Delta-9 THC along with other chemicals. More chemicals are created through the process of chemical ignition, but generally not with vaporization.

The potency of a plant can only be estimated, since even scientists have been unable to say which mix of cannabinoids and in what amount will get you the most high. Also, a marijuana high is a subjective experience. There is no way to measure how "high" someone is other than hearing him tell you how high he is. People are not affected in exactly the same way by the same amount taken from the same plant. Euphoria, elation, paranoia, sleepiness, clarity of thought – any of these may be experienced by different people pulling on the same joint. Therefore, your experiences and preferences are key and they alone should govern what you decide to plant.

Strains and Some Prime Outdoor Locations

When choosing seeds for your outdoor

grow, you should be concerned with the success that a certain strain is likely to have given your climate and location. In general, Sativa varieties will take longer to mature than pure Indica types. Also, through cloning and breeding, many varieties are available that are a cross between Indica and Sativa.

More important to consider is your climate zone: what can you expect the weather in your area to be like during the plant's growing season? Especially important to determine are the average temperature ranges at the beginning of spring and fall. Growers in tropical or southern areas tend to receive many hours of consistent sunlight throughout the growing season. Growers in northern or colder areas of the world may not have this luxury or may have to contend with other hazards. One of these is the ground still being frozen at the start of spring. Another hazard is an early winter frost, which could have an effect on potency and yield. To cope with this, growers in these areas often choose strains with shorter growing times, ensuring that their plants are out of the ground long before the first frost hits.

The marijuana plant is extremely sensitive to the quality and amount of light it receives. Once a mature plant is exposed to less than 12 hours of light each day, it will stop growing and

Think about the climate you will be growing your plant in.

Chapter 2

You need to study your plants to understand them.

Seed and Strain Selection

In a ravine we find this cluster of Lowryder by the Joint Doctor. The light was so-so, but the genetics meant that the plants had a huge yield.

devote all of its energy to flowering. In order to speed up the flowering process, some growers will move the plants if they are in pots, or cover them with opaque cloths. Artificially limiting the light received in this fashion mimics the seasonal change the plant is waiting for and tricks it into thinking that fall is nearing. In some northern areas, it might be a good idea to start flowering earlier, ensuring that you avoid the onset of an early frost, which could damage your plants' potency and yield. It might also be a good idea to plant several varieties and take advantage of their different flowering times. Plant maturity for photoperiod manipulation is generally recognized around the third or fourth week of vegetative growth after secondary branching has appeared.

The following are some general guidelines concerning regional varieties and suggested planting locations.

Regional Varieties of Marijuana

Mexican, which includes many different varieties that feature strong stems, large leaves, and different coloring, tend to do very well in equatorial zones. The plants tend to grow to a large height very quickly, which helps to avoid the early frost. This type of weed is very common in the United States for the obvious reason of proximity. It is a good smoke,

Big Laughing is a highly potent cannabis strain from celebrated breeder Dr. Greenthumb.

Mexican Sativa from Sensi Seeds is a prized cultivar from the southern province of Oaxaca, Mexico.

Delta 9's Brainstorm Haze likes warm weather and gives a huge yield with a motivating and clear high.

Super Skunk crossed with Purple Star created this amazing outdoor strain Frisian Dew from Dutch Passion.

Holland's Hope, from Dutch Passion, has a short flowering period of just eight weeks and a hard-hitting high.

Matanuska Tundra from Sagarmatha Seeds is a hybrid that produces huge buds with a chocolate aroma.

not notable for any special quality, but one that provides a consistently good high. There may be a few climate issues if you plan to grow in a northern temperate zone, since this strain of marijuana prefers warmer climes like those in the southern United States or Australia.

Hawaiian, including some varieties like Kauai and Maui, develop quickly but favor large amounts of sunlight. Though you could force-flower them through a shorter growing season, they like to soak in the sun with their large broad leaves, which help to produce huge yields of very potent marijuana. The high is strong and lasts a very long time. It tends to be clean, not leaving you feeling tired or cloudy headed. Mild climate areas like cool desert areas, coastal California and Oregon, and of course Hawaii, are recommended for growing good Hawaiian varieties.

Colombian, which has long been considered one of the best strains, has small, thin leaves supported by a slender stem. Colombian is typically grown at high altitudes where it is colder. Though the weather is cool, the country itself is tropical and therefore plants receive a lot of sunlight all year round. The climate is great for growing marijuana (or coca) but is not easily replicated in northern temperate zones. Extremely long summers with periods of sunlight more than 12 hours long until late in the growing season are required, so southern climes are better. Colombian may be difficult to grow in some areas, but if you are lucky enough to live in areas where this plant thrives outdoors, the smoke is well worth the effort.

Southeast Asian varieties like Thai or Vietnamese also have small leaves and need long growing seasons. These plants are delicate and seem to do well in warm weather. The high is great, coming on very quickly and lasting a long time. These would be unlikely to grow successfully outdoors in northern areas unless they were started inside in greenhouses and transplanted later. Experienced growers often use techniques like these that "trick" the plant into growing where it may not normally thrive.

Hybrids. There are many more strains and possible seed types. A lot of the plants that produce award-winning pot in places like Amsterdam and California are hybrids, or mixtures of various strains. If you are lucky enough to get some of these premium genetics, be sure to find out under what conditions the plant was grown, and try to replicate that environment.

The Church, a quick-flowering strain from Green House Seeds that delivers an enduring, cerebral high.

Sensi Star, an Indica-dominant variety from Paradise Seeds has very resinous, pungent buds.

Marijuana can thrive outdoors in almost any location.

Seed Storage and Labeling

To store seeds, it is best to keep them in sealed, labeled containers, in a cool, dry environment, although room temperature is also fine. They can be stored for a long time in this condition, through several growing seasons. This is something you might want to consider when labeling, since you might find that certain years produced better quality marijuana than others. The seeds themselves are very durable, and can survive being frozen for two years or more, but you shouldn't expect 100% success from seeds stored for long periods.

As with all plants, however, sometimes seeds won't germinate, or sprout. The reason may be because of improper storing, the immaturity of the seed, or something random, like a temperature fluctuation during transport.

Before planting, test some of your seeds to see if they are likely candidates. The initial stages of growth are in many ways the most important, because it might mean losing precious days of sunlight on the other end. A good test is to split a waxy, darker seed and check for a white substance with green skin inside. Alternatively, you can place a few seeds in a small cup filled ½ inch deep with dirt and soak with warm water. After the cup has been left at room temperature for about a

Seed and Strain Selection

These tall plants need stakes to support the weight of the buds.

week, seedlings should appear.

Identifying bad seeds is fairly simple. Seeds that are green or white are usually immature and will likely not germinate. If seeds crush easily in between your fingers then it is likely past the usable stage.

Always choose waxy, fat, brown seeds over their paler or darker cousins.

These are your best candidates, and the germination rate should be very high. It doesn't mean they are the only ones. Marijuana is a weed, and as such, does pretty well in the wild. Seeds scattered on the ground on their own will probably germinate as much as 25 to 40% of the time. Remember that, for whatever reason, sometimes

seeds won't grow and it is best to conduct tests a few weeks ahead of actual planting, to give yourself the best chance for a successful harvest.

Site Selection and Setups

Five to seven large, healthy, female plants can supply a heavy smoker with enough pot to last a year. This means that it only takes a relatively small area of land to provide for all of your marijuana needs. Even so, finding this space can be tricky because there are a lot of factors to consider when choosing where to grow. The ideal site would be in a secluded clearing near a riverbank with rich, rock-free soil that was blessed by the sun all day. Therein lay the four major concerns for choosing a site: security, soil, water, and light.

Where to Grow

Security

Though security will be discussed in more detail later, generally speaking, security is a top priority for any grower since plants that are "discovered" can't be harvested. If you are planting on your own property, be sure to do so in a remote area since this might give you plausible deniability. You can simply say you had no idea that it was there. Public lands that are neither hunted upon, nor near trails or other obvious attractions also make great spots. Also, watch for areas that might draw psilocybin mushroom hunters as they would love nothing more than to happen upon a stand of healthy, potent pot plants.

Another concern may be new development. There are many stories of growers scouting out a spot, prepar-ing the soil and readying their watering systems only to have the place overrun with bulldozers and workers in midsummer. Some growers use a greenhouse, even if it is just a crudely constructed greenhouse of their own design. The goal is just to conceal what's growing inside. However some people are fortunate when choosing a grow site either in that their neighbors respect their privacy or the laws in their area look kindly upon growing, and they can simply concentrate on soil, water and light.

Soil

Some people choose to plant directly into the earth while others will use a bucket or a container. Either method works well and has its drawbacks and benefits. Container planting is especially useful because you know the soil conditions and do not need to worry about preparing the site. Growers will usually create a special soil mix that will ensure that the plants receive plenty of nutrients throughout the season, so that they need only add very few, if any, additives later. Container growing also enables you to choose a site in a less accessible or hospitable area because the plants don't need to root into the earth. This

This Bubba Kush from Dr. Greenthumb is growing well in its own container with a custom soil mix.

can help you in hiding your site.

Planting directly into the earth has its advantages because there may be many more nutrients available if the soil is good. In addition, your plants can root very deeply and grow extremely large since they won't be limited by their nutrients or the size of the container. One problem is that you may have to prepare the location as much as a year in advance, tilling soil, and changing the pH of the existing soil. The benefit is that a little work goes a long way. Also, since you're putting them directly into the earth, the extra nutrients won't be washed away as easily from rain or with watering, and will remain around for the roots to use them as needed. Either way, make sure you're giving your plant good nutrient-rich, balanced soil.

Water

Sites that are located near water sources that will not dry up during the summertime are especially important. Bringing in buckets of water to your plant site may not be the best idea since it is hard to conceal your actions and you may arouse suspicion. River beds are often good sites but since rivers attract people, as well as insects and animals who may wish to nibble on your leaves, planting downhill from a river may be a better option. This way you can irrigate your plants by doing something as simple as running an ordinary length of garden hose from the river to your plants. Bear in mind though, that the pH of the river should be tested since it may change throughout the course of the summer, or may not be suitable for use in the first place. In general a pH of 7 is what outdoor cannabis likes best.

If you receive a lot of summer rain, you can catch some of that water in a large submerged barrel or tank and irrigate from that as well. Rainwater is generally well balanced though in heavily industrial areas it may be too acidic. There are also more expensive and fancy means that involve pumps, timers, and drip systems. If the best possible site option you have requires one of these, you may be forced to give it some consideration.

Light

Finally, your last consideration is how much light your site receives—ideally, as much as possible. The amount of light your plant receives will be directly related to how successful your harvest is. Planting in the woods, usually the first choice for novice growers, can be bad in this respect because the plants will have to compete with much taller

This garden, started in the cold spring, was a homemade greenhouse.

These marijuana plants are getting all the sunlight they need which is evident from their abundant leaf production.

trees for light. Look for a place that gets optimal amounts of morning light and additional sun throughout the day. Finding proper light is often the hardest task in site choosing because these well-lit areas tend to be noticeable or well-trafficked. Choose wisely and remember that as a minimum five hours of direct light, with many more hours of indirect sunlight, is your target.

All of this underscores that forethought is required in order to have a successful harvest. Thoroughly investigate a number of sites and plant in more than one location. This way you'll have backup but more importantly, you'll discover which location is the best and where you should focus your efforts in the future. Planning goes a long way, and later, when you're relaxing with the fruits of your labor, it will all be worth it.

Basic Lighting Needs

Marijuana is a sun-loving plant and will easily grow to large heights if provided with enough solar contact. But since it is also a durable and resilient plant, growers have been able to successfully obtain buds from plants grown with only a skylight.

Sunlight encourages leaf and stem production, which in turn enables the plant to retain more sunlight, ultimately leading to more growth and a larger yield. If your plants don't receive adequate sunlight, no amount of soil and water preparation will compensate for this crucial deficiency.

While light is necessary for growth, it is darkness that actually triggers flowering in mature plants. Once a mature plant receives a certain minimum amount of uninterrupted darkness for a week or so, this signals to the plant that the growing season has ended. The mature plant will begin to convert its energy from growing to flowering. This is why it is best to grow your plants as early in the spring as possible, so that they receive the maximum amount of light, and can therefore spend most of their life cycle growing.

It is best to try and plant in a spot where your plants will receive sunlight for the longest possible period of time. Midway through the growing season, when the days are longest, the sun can be shining for 12 or more hours a day. Your goal is to find a location such as a clearing, free of trees or other obstacles that could prevent your plant's leaves from capturing the sun's rays and using them to power growth.

South-facing sites are usually the best in the northern hemisphere and vice versa for those in the southern hemisphere. This may not be possible for everyone due to other concerns like security or perhaps access to water. In that case make sure your plant receives at least five hours of direct sunlight and

This Church from Green House Seed Co. is receiving plenty of sun and has only a couple more weeks to go until harvest.

This Iranian Short Season from Dr. Greenthumb will be ready to harvest in August.

five hours of indirect sunlight each day. If you must choose between morning sun and afternoon sun then the consensus is that morning sun is best for growth.

Some northern growers experience a different problem: darkness plays a large factor in northern regions. Since the nights are short, the plants may not have enough time to flower before autumn sets in and, with it, the first frost. For these growers, being able to simulate a longer night to trigger flowering may be necessary. In this case a greenhouse or other enclosure may be the only way to grow outside. Please note that the darkness must be total as any light the plants receive, even if only briefly, will stall flowering and restart vegetative growth.

Growers near the equator or in other southerly places with long periods of darkness (more than ten hours for consecutive nights) may find that their plants flower too soon. This is a lot easier to deal with since shining light is always easier than withholding.

Either way, it is important to remember that light, because it is important to both the vegetative growth and flowering stages, should be looked at from the perspective of the plant's entire life cycle. One of the great advantages to growing outdoors is that, providing that you have picked a great spot for the plants, the sun and changing seasons should do the rest.

Being close to a natural source of water is a big plus.

A constant supply of water is essential for your grow.

Basic Watering Needs

Marijuana requires a fair amount of water to live and thrive, though calculating the exact amount is nearly impossible without factoring in basics like soil, climate, and the intensity of light, as well as the time of year, strain type, and the stage of the growth cycle. For instance, some tall, healthy plants may require several gallons of water a day during the hottest months, others, much less.

Since a plant can only consume a certain amount of water, a plant that gets 25 to 40 gallons of supplemental water will grow to the exact same size and yield as a plant that receives an infinite amount. It is important therefore to watch for signs telling you what your crop's water needs are. If a plant is underwatered, it will stop growing, the leaves will dry and wilt, and eventually it may die, however overwatering a plant can produce the same symptoms, checking the dampness of the soil is the way to tell the difference, sometimes digging down slightly with a trowel to find hidden reserves of water where the sun has only dried the surface. In general if the soil remains fairly damp four days after the last time you watered, you will not need to feed it additional water.

When your plants are seedlings, maintaining moist soil through frequent watering is necessary. After a month or two, the soil should be allowed to dry in between waterings. This lets some of the roots come in contact with the air. As they grow, your plants will develop good, deep roots, enabling them to tap into underground sources of moisture and nutrients. The roots will simply follow the moisture wherever it leads. This underground moisture will also make it difficult to tell when older plants need water. In general, you can plan on watering the area once a week—more if you are in an especially sunny area,

This raised bed grow means that there are less weeds and it will keep out some pests that love to nibble on your plants. They also provide better drainage and your back will thank you.

Be prepared to amend your soil by adding fertilizers and nutrients to ensure the best possible results.

which is drying out the soil.

Another reason you may have to water your plants frequently is if the soil is quite porous. This type of soil is found in western states like California, Arizona, and New Mexico. Unless your growing site is located near a water source, like a river or stream, regions with this type of soil also tend to have a low groundwater level. The combination of porous soil and low groundwater level make the need for extra water even more important.

Basic Soil Requirements

The soil in which you plant your seeds is obviously going to play a large part in how well your plants grow and what you'll eventually harvest. Ideally, the best soil would be fluffy when held in your hands, would drain well, and would be rich in nutrients. If you are planting your seeds in large pots, then this is easier to come by since you can either compost or buy fertilizer that provides a rich fertile base in which to plant. If you're planting in a more

natural location, a bit of preparation and testing is required to make the soil more amenable for your grow. Either way marijuana requires a lot of certain nutrients throughout its life in order to produce a high yield. The less nutrients, light, or water, the less you harvest. The three basic nutrients are nitrogen (N), potassium (P) and phosphorous (K). Any store-bought fertilizer should show the percentages of each in large numbers on the front of the packaging, and they are always listed in N-P-K order. These nutrients must always be available for your seedlings to grow into strong, healthy, mature plants.

The challenge to you, the grower, is to balance and maintain these nutrients in the soil throughout the course of the plant's life. This may be easier if you are using store-bought fertilizer and planting in pots because the mix may already be pH balanced (pH 7, neither too acidic nor overly alkaline). Even so, the plants may begin to exhibit deficiencies in one or more of the nutrients because the plants do not use them up evenly. In that case you'll have to supplement the exhausted nutrients, either through watering or through feeding them directly to the soil. The plant's look and feel will be a signal as to which nutrients you may be short on. One of the main drawbacks to planting in pots is that you are responsible for providing all of the nutrients that the plant needs, since the roots will not be able to seek them out in the existing soil. Also the size of the pot, which in turn regulates how much soil you are growing the plant in, will regulate how tall and strong the plant can grow. The benefit to planting in pots is that you are in control of all the nutrients that the plant could possibly receive.

If you are planting in a pot there are a few things to keep in mind concerning the container. Growers have used a wide variety of containers, but a good general rule is, the lighter the better, in case you have to move your plants. Five-gallon (about nineteen litres) plastic buckets, which are the ubiquitous by-product of restaurants, work well as long they haven't been used to store petroleum or anything toxic or heavily acidic. Clay pots are heavy, needlessly costly, and actually absorb moisture that should be used by your plants. If you use them, be sure to spray the pot itself with water whenever you water, especially during the hot summer months. Gardening stores also sell grow bags which are thick enough to hold a good amount of soil, and durable in case you need to move them; however, be extremely careful when moving them since the jostling could damage the roots. This will disrupt the plant's ability to grow as it must tend to and rebuild its ailing root system. Make sure you have drainage holes in the bottom of your container so that excess water won't drown your plants, but they shouldn't be so big that soil falls out. Another tip is to put a few rocks or something else solid within the soil that will help with drainage, but don't overdo it.

If you are growing directly in the natural soil it is best to have a basic understanding of what kind of soil you

A nice, healthy balanced soil that is ready for planting.

This heavy clay soil will need a healthy addition of fertilizer before anything is planted.

Sandy soil drains quickly so try adding compost.

This Sour Diesel is ripe and ready to harvest.

have and what else is growing nearby. There are three main types of soil: clay, sandy, and loamy. A good way to determine what kind of soil you are dealing with is to ask a local gardening store what type of soil is common to the area, or simply grab a handful and show it to them. It will usually be a mixture of one or more of the following types, leaning more toward one or the other.

Clay soils are heavy soils and densely packed. They hold water well, but don't let the air move freely and can therefore inhibit root growth. Clay soils are found everywhere in the world and should not be planted into directly unless you have suitably prepared them. Digging big planting holes several feet in diameter and adding a compost mix or a good fertilizer is your best bet.

Sandy soils, on the other hand, are found near oceans and coastal areas, in more arid areas and over many inland regions. Light, sandy soils allow for root penetration and air movement, which is necessary since minerals are not readily available and the roots might have to search them out. Another characteristic is that water moves quickly through the soil and is not held very long. In order to improve on sandy soils so that your plants have the best chance to grow large in size and yield well is to prepare the soil extensively. A mixture of damp, humid compost can help stiffen and bind the soil together, enabling it to retain water and enhance nutrient uptake. Also, because coastal

The local soil here is too acidic, so the grower grows in pots filled with good soil.

areas tend to be warmer, you might need to add some loose fertilizer into the mix and perhaps some planter's mulch, which should keep the temperature of the soil cooler than the surrounding area.

Loamy soils are fertile and drain well. They are moist enough to trap the nutrients your plant needs to thrive, but have enough air between particles so that the roots stay healthy. They hold water and moisture like clay, but allow movement similar to sandy soils. Store-bought fertilizer imitates this basic soil composition. In order to achieve a more well-balanced soil, you would have to compost. However, just because your soil is naturally loamy doesn't mean that it will stay nutrient-rich throughout the plant's life. You may still need to add nutrients during the vegetative growth stage of the plant's life cycle.

Soil Testing

Since all soils are a mixture of loamy, sandy, and clay derivation, figuring out which kind of soil you have is the first step to preparing your soil. Testing its exact makeup is the second step; preparing the area with either compost or fertilizer is the last. Testing is very important even if you are planting in containers or pots filled with store-bought fertilizer. While most are pH balanced and will tell you so on the packaging, some potting soils are notoriously acidic. In order to test the makeup of the soil you should get a pH tester.

The pH level is tested on a scale from 1 to 14 that measures the acid-to-alkaline balance, 1 being the most acidic, 7 being neutral, and 14 being the most alkaline. Every point change equates to a tenfold increase or decrease in acidity or alkalinity. Therefore soil with a pH of 5 is 10 times more acidic than soil with a pH of 6 and soil with a pH of 5 is 100 times more acidic than water with a pH of 7.

Cannabis grows best in soil with a pH between 6.5 and 7. This is the range in which the plants can absorb all of the required nutrients most efficiently. If the pH is too low (acidic), salts block nutrient intake or prevent the plants from breaking them down, thus keeping the nutrients from the roots. Toxic salt buildup might also limit the roots' ability to take in water. An alkaline soil may cause nutrients to become unavailable to the plant as well, or to not break down in the soil, instead being flushed away during the next watering. During the vegetative growth stage, soil that tests more alkaline (7.1–7.4) may help the plant depending on your soil conditions and on whether other nutrients are added as needed. Once the plant begins its flowering process though, the soil should be as close to 7 as possible.

There are three main devices used to measure pH—soil test kits, litmus paper, and electronic pH testers—all of which are available at most gardening or home improvement stores. When testing pH, take two or three samples and follow the instructions supplied by the manufacturer to the letter. The kits measure the soil's pH and primary nutrient content by mixing soil with a chemical solution. This produces a color that you then compare to a chart. Be sure that you understand how it works and if necessary, test it on soil that you already know to be balanced. Electronic testers are the most clear, precise, and easy to use and will give you the most consistent results

Fertilizers and Composting

The composition of the soil that your plant lives in is obviously going to influence your harvest. There is one major decision for choosing that soil and your choice will probably depend on your situation and the amount of effort you are willing to put in. The first option is using a store-bought (or chemical) fertilizer; the second is going organic and/or composting; and the third option is just throwing your seeds anywhere and seeing what happens. Each of these could work but the organic route is the one that I recommend, and you'll be able to see, smell and, most importantly, feel and taste the difference.

Using a store-bought or chemical soil is a good option for people who can't or won't invest the maximum time in their plants. Many first-time growers use this option since there are fewer variables to consider. The soil is prepackaged and often sold with instructions or tips for growing. Chemical fertilizers contain all of the essential nutrients and the packaging should tell you in what quantities these nutrients are present. Growers who use containers or pots will most often choose this route since the amount of soil they need to treat is limited, and they need to make sure that the roots receive the necessary nutrients.

Even though the soil is sold ready to use and complete, it is still necessary to test throughout the season since the pH may change. Another reason to check the pH is that some store-bought soils are unusually acidic. Either way, you may find that you need to add extra nutrients to your soil depending on the condition of your plants. It is for this reason that experienced growers who start off with chemical soil will still use organic soil amendments.

The most often encountered reason for growing organically is that there is almost a zero chance that you will burn the plants. Too much chemical fertilizer can be a bad thing, since it is highly concentrated and may leave salts behind in the soil. The roots rapidly absorb the chemical fertilizers and, like someone who eats

Sour Diesel is a great strain for outdoors and produces dense, thick buds.

too quickly, will experience a negative reaction. This could include the death of your plants. Usually what happens is that too much of one nutrient prevents the uptake of others, leaving your plant deficient and dying. When fed organic substances, plants will only take in the nutrients they need, leaving the rest in the soil. The remaining nutrients are broken down slowly, which ensures a steady supply.

The major drawback to organic growing is the knowledge needed and the preparation that may be necessary to deliver the nutrients to the plants. Composting takes time and should be started months in advance. It requires a space in which to accomplish this, preferably far away from people since it can carry quite an odor. Also, depending on your security needs, it may be impossible to get the composted soil to the grow site, since where you compost and where you grow may be very far apart. In cases like these it is best to add individual organic matter to the existing site and bring that soil up to par.

The idea behind composting is that organic matter decays with the help of bacteria created in the decomposition process into a brown, loose blend called humus. This is the same process that natural soil uses, though in nature it takes much longer. You accelerate this process through composting because the mixture of things added increases the presence and activity of bacteria and microorganisms. In good, fertile soil there are untold millions of microorganisms in every gram, as well as earthworms, which are attracted to good soil and improve it by living within it. Composting is just a way of duplicating the conditions and qualities of good soil. It is easy since it relies on your waste products, things that you were going to rid yourself of anyway, such as green grass clippings, leaves, fish scraps, dried flowers, bones, anything vegetable from your kitchen that you don't eat like corncobs, plant skins, et cetera. Meats and animal fat should not be composted as they create a haven for maggots and parasites that do nothing to help create healthy, fertile soil. Most manure is great, except from pets (dogs and cats), and some people recommend against pine needles since they decrease the pH and take a long time to break down anyway.

When composting, try to shred everything you put into the pile because

These young plants are enjoying the benefits of growing in a true organic soil.

that speeds the process greatly. It is as much an art as it is a science in that there are as many different ways to do it as there are reasons for it being done. Just remember that layering your piles is important, and preventing the circulation of air within the pile is bad. There are numerous informational sites on the Web, as well as books that offer various tips. Remember that you can pH test the compost and add lime or bonemeal to change the pH in either direction. Since most of us do not live on farms, gathering a good mix of organic items won't happen in a short period of time. This is it why it may take months to make a good mix. But once accomplished, your composting efforts will have created much better soil than is available in most garden stores.

Because even chemical growers will likely need to augment their soil, here is a partial list of some organic additives that can enhance the soil quality. This is by no means exhaustive as growers have been known to add all kinds of things, but this should get you through most seasons. For a more complete list there are many online or print resources, some of which are listed in the resources section of this book. Some of these will even tell you the exact ratios of nitrogen, potassium and phosphorus contained in each and when in the season they may be most appropriate.

Amending Soil

Correcting soil deficiencies before planting will greatly increase the likely success of your plants. For the example photographed here, we have chosen a sandy site.

To correct the composition of the soil, we have added organic compost, bone meal and peat moss. Using a pitchfork to combine the amendments allows you to break up the soil as you mix, allowing for the roots of your plants to expand quickly and easily.

Organic Additives

Blood meal has a very high concentration of nitrogen and is therefore a popular choice for the vegetative growth period.

Bone meal is high in phosphorus, and is most suitable for the flowering period. It is a slow-release fertilizer so most growers add it during the later stages of the vegetative growth stage.

Fish emulsion is a liquid solution made mainly from decomposed fish and

Soil amendments can improve your soil but unnecessary and over-use can backfire and create more problems. Even organic materials can cause problems if used incorrectly. Increasing the soil pH can create a nutrient imbalance while lowering the pH can create toxic conditions.

other ingredients. Most growers use this when their plants are still young as it is gentle and provides a nice balance of nutrients.

Worm castings may be the best all-purpose fertilizer. While not being high in any one nutrient they contain micronutrients, which aid the soil generally, and a very balanced mixture of the three basic nutrients (N-P-K).

Kelp meal is best when used as part of the general soil or composting mix as it is rich in many elements and ensures an abundance of micronutrients.

Manures. These are a mixed lot, with the excrement of different animals having slightly different effects. In general though, rabbit, cow, chicken, horse, and bat manure provide excellent bases for any composting mix but should not be added directly to soil.

Coffee grounds are highly acidic and are generally used to rapidly change the pH of soil or compost.

Eggshells when ground down are another often used household substance that is great in the compost pile. They usually have an alkaline affect.

Lime is sworn upon by many organic growers as a quick way to raise the pH and render formerly acidic soil alkaline. Other growers though dismiss it since it takes a while to break down and cause the reaction. This is probably best added to compost or early in the season if you have good reason to believe your

soil might need an alkaline boost.

Wood ashes work very quickly to raise the pH, are high in micronutrients and are, in general, just good for the soil.

No matter which soil base you choose, remember that once your plants have begun to flower, you should flush the soil with water. This rids the soil of excess nutrients and greatly enhances the taste and size of your harvest. If you are using store-bought fertilizers it is, generally speaking, a good idea to flush your plants every three to four weeks. Check the pH levels at least once a week for the first month after planting your seedlings, and twice per week after that or any time something seems amiss. Marijuana does a good job of letting you know when something is wrong since it will discolor, droop, or lose excessive amounts of leaves. If your soil mix is good though, that is just one less thing to worry about during the growing season.

Using Other Plants as a Guide

No matter which hemisphere you are planting in, marijuana will grow during the summer months when the sun is longest in the sky and the nights are short. Looking at the growth cycles of other plants in your area can benefit the savvy grower in two main ways. First, it can help you gather information about your growing climates since

Niagara x Shiva from Dr. Greenthumb is an incredible plant for growers and smokers alike.

the harvest times for these plants are similar and you should typically plant around the same time. Some examples of typical summer plants are corn (the best guide) and tomatoes. There are also myriad plants and bushes that need to be started early in the spring. You can't approach a garden store

asking specifically about your plants, but you can hide your real reason for asking. For instance, a conversation with an employee might clue you into subtle facts about the season's rainfall, or pests that you might not have considered. Also, he may inadvertently tip you off about good or poor sites,

since he should have good knowledge of the local conditions. Granted this information won't be 100% transferable, but it should give you a good baseline.

Secondly, if you find a plant that is green and grows to a tall height (or even one that isn't green) it may help you camouflage your own plants. A popular grower trick, particularly for those growing in urban areas, is to attach flowers to their marijuana plants throughout the season to imitate a local plant. The flowers are tied on loosely but the effect works when seen from say, the street below or a helicopter overhead. One grower whose plants were on his balcony used this method in conjunction with tying down some branches. Along the rim of the balcony were planters with jasmine, spider plants, and other leafy green plants that created a lush sensation. When seen from below it looked as if he merely had a green thumb. Other growers will plant bushes or maybe even bamboo to create an environmental shield around the plant site contained within. This won't work though, if your plants soon outgrow the smaller protective barrier. Marijuana grows rapidly and will shoot upwards if it thinks it needs to in order to capture the maximum amount of sunlight. Therefore, don't plant your own plants too close together, and definitely don't plant your shield too close. It will be self-defeating.

Basically, keeping in mind what else grows in your environment can be useful. Either it will aid in your plants' being healthier and stronger, or it will prevent them from being stolen or seized. Remember, what you are growing is part of the ecosystem you are working within so any information you can get about local plants may help.

Security Issues
Hiding Your Plants from Prying Eyes
Security issues vary widely from country to country and even within distinct regions of a particular country. Growers in Vancouver seem to have less problem growing outdoors than growers in the southwestern United States. Hawaiian growers often have to engage in large amounts of subterfuge whereas Australians have the luxury of space and generally unconcerned neighbors.

The first step in protecting yourself is to know the laws and penalties in your area, so that you can decide if this is a risk worth taking. Some states in the United States have a zero-tolerance law that assigns harsh minimum penalties (jail time, fines, et cetera) for even one measly leaf, whereas in some countries in the EU

This NYC Diesel from Soma is coming along nicely and will provide this balcony grower with a great harvest.

This dense grow site provides good natural cover for the grower's small patch.

and in some states, notably California, the amount needed before you face the threat of prosecution can be quite large. Often the authorities will seize your stash and fine you, before letting you go. As a general rule of thumb, the fewer people you tell the better chance you have of harvesting those plants. In fact the best practice is to not tell anyone anything at all.

In the United States, police find hundreds of thousands of cannabis plants annually using aerial surveillance and infrared photography. Many communities receive federal funds to eradicate cannabis crops, but it is important to note that they are looking mainly for large plots which are easier to spot than small personal gardens. Depending on the laws in your state,

some police departments will confiscate all of your property and auction it off in order to buy new hi-tech surveillance equipment, firearms, vehicles and other toys with which to continue their quest to destroy cannabis plants and the people who grow them.

Security should be the number one concern in site preparation. Well-concealed gardens are harvested,

Growing only a few plants in a space will minimize the danger of the grow being targeted by thieves.

detected plants are not. Again, a good idea is to select a site away from your own property or in a remote location where people are not often spotted hunting, hiking, or passing through. Use the plants around the site for coverage, and if necessary plant some nearby which will help to mask your own.

Try to plant under trees or next to bushes, and keep only a few plants in any one spot. That way if some are discovered you'll still have others to harvest. Through bending and pruning you can change the classic conical shape of the plants into something that might be mistaken for mere foliage. Plus, when you bend the stems horizontally, it can help to give more sun to growing buds, making your yield even larger. Plants can be grown under trees, but remember that they need at least five hours of direct light and as much indirect light as possible. Some growers have been known to pin flowers to their plants to help in the disguise. Another method is to grow near other plants that are close in color or size to your plants. Be careful though, because if these plants begin to wither and die, during the end of the summer growing season, your plants will stand out like a spotlight.

Make sure your plants are out of sight from casual onlookers and try to take a different route to get to them each time you visit the site. When you visit your plants you might want to cover your tracks and try not to unsettle the environment too much. When seen from above, your different paths to the same place will have a bicycle wheel effect, focusing attention on the place where all the paths stop. Also, try to park near other cars even if it means taking a longer route to your plants. This is one reason why it is important to have a water source nearby. It is hard to look inconspicuous when toting a large amount of water into a remote area. Always have a good reason for being in the area and have the necessary items to make your claim believable.

These are some of the many contingencies that you must prepare for and think about well before you begin germinating. Sometimes it might be necessary to think small at first and grow fewer plants that you can be sure you will be able to harvest.

It can't be said too many times: the most basic thing that you can do to protect your crop is to be very guarded about who you tell. If you must reveal its existence, never, ever disclose the location. If your site is well hidden then usually the reason you get ripped off or reported is because you bragged about your plants. If your plants are cut down or discovered, then it doesn't matter how big they are or how much time you put in, because they won't be there for you to harvest.

Growing your marijuana amongst other varieties of plants can help conceal your grow.

Guerrilla Farming

Guerrilla farming, as the name implies, refers to the clandestine efforts that most outdoor growers have to utilize in order to successfully harvest each year. Due to the increasingly aggressive efforts of the authorities in some areas, growers have been forced to use ingenious methods. Some hide their plants by interspersing them with other crops. Some growers have been able to grow plants amongst the branches of trees. Others utilize abandoned buildings and stealthily grow on rooftops. Some of these locations have severe drawbacks, because, while they may be safe from police seizure, they are not easily accessible for watering or other cultivation needs like pruning and pest control. For example, growers who use small, barely reachable patches on hillsides and the like are sometimes forced to carry water to each individual plant.

The main idea behind guerrilla growing, though, is to prevent the plants from being discovered, and most importantly, to prevent that discovery from being traced back to you.

Heighten Security During Harvest

Until the harvest, security is mainly a matter of diverting unwanted attention away from your plants. All of this changes as the flowering period ebbs, because now you must concern yourself with your actual yield. In this situation, growers have been known to resort to some very elaborate and even over-the-top means to protect their buds from prying eyes. While some will sleep near their "babies" for the days immediately leading up to the harvest, others will set up trip wire that rings a bell if anyone approaches. If their site is close to home, they might keep a dog that barks a lot outside all night. Other growers simply watch the known entrance routes like a hawk. During these days the growers are irritable, cranky, and extra paranoid, but with a year's supply (or oftentimes, even more) of cannabis at stake, can you really blame them?

It is also important to remember that all of the other security concerns

Don't bring bags like these!

Even legal grows must be aware of security.

Strains that don't grow tall can help you conceal your grow.

still apply and the same level of care (if not more) should be taken. It is not unusual for plants to be staked out by potential thieves who are waiting for them to grow big buds so they can reap the benefits of your time and effort. The police could also have detected your plot weeks ago and be waiting for you to walk into a trap that you yourself have unwittingly set. When you show up at your site with shears, bags, and a backpack, it is hard to claim ignorance. Therefore it is important to do the following things: pick as secure a grow site as possible, and if you suspect that something is wrong, relax and walk away. After all, it's just marijuana, it is not worth going to jail, or getting into a fight about.

4

Chapter 4

The Grow

Growing marijuana outdoors is as inherently natural as growing tomatoes, corn, or tulips. The plant thrives untended in the wild and has also been cultivated all over the world for centuries. Outdoors, nature provides most of what the plant will need and the grower's job is simply to enhance the plant's chances for reaching its full potential. That said, in order to ensure a successful grow, knowledge of certain fundamentals is necessary.

Getting Started

The growing season runs from spring to fall; however in colder areas, it is shortened at both the beginning and end. Your plants can be started at any time, but planting early does allow for taller plants with stronger branches that can support larger yields. Larger plants are a combination of high yielding genetics and optimal growing conditions. The most important thing is to start with good genetics.

Germination Techniques

There are several different methods to consider when starting your crop. I will describe three: planting and spacing in rows, broadcast seeding, and indoor germination. This beginning stage of marijuana growth is very similar to that of most houseplants. A smart grower will take advantage of this fact, by utilizing one of many germination

and transplanting techniques that are readily available on the market. Nurseries and hardware stores will usually employ qualified people who can help you select the best pots and give you tips suited to your environment, using tomatoes as your example. The Internet is also a great resource for growers.

Planting and Spacing in Rows

Planting your seeds directly outdoors can be beneficial because the plants will not have to suffer any of the ill effects of transplanting. If you have already prepared the soil—either through composting, or by creating raised beds of good, balanced soil—and the seeds you have chosen are from good stock, this is a quick way to get started.

Using a hoe, plow, or tiller, construct a series of rows two to six feet apart. Rows are convenient to use, especially in large areas, but require tending. The general orientation of your rows must also take into account the sun requirements of your plants. As a rule, rows should face in a southeasterly direction to allow both sides of your plants to capture the sun's nourishing rays.

To plant, simply place a few seeds into holes spaced about four to eight inches apart, and sprinkle the soil with water. If the soil is very dry, you may want to consider returning for another watering session two to three days later. In a short time the plants will have germinated and this sprouting can take up to four weeks to occur. At this point, water them every day and monitor their development closely. Some of the faster growing ones may crowd out or shade the smaller ones. You might want to remove the smaller

Freshly sprouted seedling.

shoots and replant them where they will receive more sun. At this stage in their development, replanting won't affect plants too much. The plants may experience transplant shock, however, and so very careful attention should be paid in the first few days following transplantation, including staking, ensuring good light, and keeping the soil well watered.

Broadcast Seeding

Broadcast seeding is a good way to make your plants blend into the environment but is a poor use of seeds. In broadcast seeding, seeds are tossed or shaken onto prepared soil in a haphazard way. After you have sown the area, simply press the seeds down to cover them with soil, using your hands or feet. Make sure that your seeds are covered since exposure to the sun may cause them to dry out and die. If your soil is made of compost or fertilizer and contains the necessary nutrients for growth, then this method should be fine, and it is certainly a lot quicker than planting in rows.

This method relies on the plant's natural ability for growth under adverse and extreme conditions. By comparison, your nicely tended-to area will be a plant paradise, and the germination and the creation of sprouts should not be a problem.

Indoor Germination: Growing in Pots

The most intensive and thorough method of starting plants and producing seedlings involves germinating the plants indoors. For best results, start with a high-quality potting container, available from any hardware or gardening store, and fill with a mixture of soil or compost and sand. Sand is essential because it helps with drainage and allows the roots to penetrate and grow, encouraging them to become strong enough to take hold when the plant is eventually moved outdoors.

Plant the seeds, one per pot, and water them thoroughly for the next few days but don't overdo it. Make sure that the soil stays moist but stop watering if water starts to pool at the base of the pot. This is a signal that you have delivered more water than the soil, or composting mixture, can hold. The roots can only absorb so much water and too much water is almost as severe a problem as too little.

Other Container Options

You can start plants in any container

that will hold them, such as milk cartons that have been cut in half or traditional flowerpots. Peat pots are recommended for growing seedlings because they can be placed directly into the soil when it's time for transplanting. An additional benefit of peat pots is that the roots will grow directly through the pot, making it abundantly clear when it is time to transplant. Seedlings grown in milk cartons or traditional flowerpots have to be removed from their containers prior to transplanting. When doing this, you must be as careful as possible not to damage the young rootlets.

Transplanting and Moving Plants

At this point all of your pots filled with freshly planted seeds are being kept indoors—either in a closet under fluorescent lights or another cool, well-lit place. Once the first sprouts begin to shoot up, move them out to the sun, either into a greenhouse or directly under the sunlight. After two weeks, the plants should have developed roots strong enough to be transplanted into your prepared soil.

It is also at this point that a smart grower will practice some sex selection, choosing to transplant only the females. Sexing marijuana plants is discussed in detail in the next section.

Generally speaking, transplanting should be done either after the first

Successful transplants.

frost or sometime after the first day of spring if your area has mild weather. Try to do it on a rainy or cloudy day, as the small plants will have an easier time adjusting to the new environment without the added pressure of intense sunlight.

If you started your plants in a greenhouse, or under fluorescent lights, they may require a two-week period of hardening and may display evidence of shock from possible transplants. A sure sign of shock is a stem collapse or wilting.

One way to ward off the adverse effects of a transplant is to move your seedlings into a partially sunny spot for a few days before the transplant. This is like weaning them to the sun and, if they receive a few hours of sunlight, it can greatly ease the effects of being under the sun for the 10 to 12 hours they will soon be receiving.

In preparation for transplanting, you can score your pots with a knife, or other instrument, to make holes that the roots can penetrate. If you are using peat pots, you will be able to see root penetration clearly. In order for your plants to be strong enough to handle the months ahead, these roots will have to multiply and harden. Creating additional holes can make this easier, and enables the plant to weather the growing season.

Before transplanting, water the area you are transplanting to and the plant, then dig a hole a bit larger than the pot and loosen the surrounding soil. Place the entire peat pot into the hole and pack the soil so that the stem base is at the same depth that it was growing at before. Firmly press the soil and water the area again. If you are using traditional flowerpots or milk cartons, you should carefully remove the entire plant and soil from the pot. Then proceed as described above.

Be certain to only move the plants that are the tallest, and look the most fit. Unless you have an unlimited amount of space, it doesn't make sense to transplant the plants that are struggling, or seem very weak. Though these might eventually recover and grow well, make sure you transplant the strongest first. Also, if security or other factors cause you to have many different growing sites, it might be best to mix your best plants with the others at the various locations.

One grower in Georgia told me that, except at his most secure site, he never plants more than one excellent plant at each site. Each site consists of five plants, scattered around a national park. Since the chance of his plants being ripped off or discovered and destroyed is high, he figures this is the best way to limit his liability. At his most secure site, where he has been growing without a problem for six seasons, he plants only the best of each year's seedlings. He usually does not transplant the weaker ones, reserving them for his indoor crop. The amount of attention they require makes them unlikely to survive in the wild, and indoor growing is the only way to ensure a good harvest from them.

The type of soil at the site you have chosen will determine whether you decide to dig a hole, or plant in raised beds. If the soil doesn't drain well, is hard clay or rocks, or has poor nutrients, then a raised bed might be preferable. If you are digging holes, be sure to dig them at least 18 inches deep, about 2 to 3 feet apart. Loosely fill the hole with your fertilizer or compost and any decaying matter available. Marijuana, like most plants, responds well to the minerals released as organic matter decays.

Mix the filling well, before putting some of the original soil back to raise the area a few inches. Depending on the soil, you may want to raise the soil as much as a foot. During the growing season it will settle down. It is important though, that the soil be loose, as otherwise the roots may exert too much energy trying to penetrate the soil, which can retard growth. If soil preparation is done about a month before the growing season starts, when the time comes to transplant, the soil will be a perfect environment for your plants.

The Grow

Outdoor Transplanting

1. Place rocks on bottom.

2. Fill ¾ of pot with soil.

3. Thoroughly water soil.

4. Create a hole for plant.

5. Gently remove plant from old pot.

6. Prod soil to loosen the roots.

7. Place plant in new pot.

8. Tamp down soil to secure plant.

9. Water regularly.

Sexing Your Plants

Why Sexing Is Important, in a Nutshell:

• Male plants don't get you as high.
• Pollinated females produce less bud. Enough said.

How to Grow all Females

The sex of your plants is genetically determined but is also influenced by the environment. The cannabis plant has two pairs of sex chromosomes, one of which carries the genes that determine sex. As with humans, these are either X or Y. Male plants have the XY chromosome while females are XX. In nature, each grouping has a roughly 50:50 chance of occurring per seed, but in your garden you can control male to female ratios once you learn to recognize what each gender looks like.

Identifying Males

Male marijuana plants usually start to flower one to four weeks sooner than females. They develop fewer flowers and tend to grow straight up, with flowers developing near the top. The immature first flowers (preflowers), appear at the tips of the main stem and branches. These flowers are usually closed, green, and develop in tight clusters. The main parts of the male

Male flowers, the pollen sacks hang like little balls.

A female plant with the pistils emerging from the calyx.

flower are five petal-shaped objects that enclose the sex organs. They look like a tiny bunch of bananas. As it matures, each one of these clusters opens to reveal a stamen. Stamens allow the plants to produce pollen that is used for reproduction in the wild.

The best way to identify a male is by looking at the preflowers, the calyx, during the early stages of growth. If the calyx is raised on a small stalk or stem then it is generally a male. If the calyx is not raised then it is generally a female. Watch these areas closely as they develop to learn the difference.

Identifying Females

Female marijuana flowers, which start to appear later than those of the males, look more like sacks. As they develop, two upraised feather-like stigmas will shoot out of each sack. They are usually white or cream-colored and are generally found on the main stalk at a node region. A node region is the area on a plant where a branch grows from the stem or where a branch grows on a branch. These stalks are designed to trap the pollen released by the male plant and carried along by the wind.

A Word About Pollination

If a female plant should receive pollen, it will no longer focus its energy on growing flowers, but will instead start to produce seeds. A healthy female

Container of pollen from a cannabis plant.

plant can produce a lot of seeds, but unless you are trying to breed a particular type of marijuana, seed production will offer you no benefits. For this reason, growers remove male plants as soon as they identify them. Another reason to remove the males is that this will give your remaining female plants more sun and light, and will also reduce the number of plants you are tending. Male plants are not very good to smoke, but leaving them in the ground (away from your females) is fine, because you can still use the leaves to make potent pot butter.

Removing Males from Your Growing Site

Uprooting male plants from the ground is one extremely reliable way to eliminate the males from your crop. Simply remove the plant and the

You can force your female plants to flower by manipulating their light intake.

day. Soon flowers will have appeared at the nodes, or joints. It should be apparent which flowers are males and which are females.

Remove the male plants, and select the strongest healthy female plants to be transplanted to your growing site. Before moving them outside, give the plants at least three days of continuous light. This will stop the plant from continuing to blossom—you do not want your females flowering too early. Once the plant is outside, receiving the long hours of natural sunlight, it will return to a vegetative state, devoting all of its energy to growing taller and stronger.

Both of the above methods will help you limit the amount of seeds or prevent seed production entirely, as well as reduce or eliminate the presence of male plants however force flowering can sometimes cause sexual dysfunction to appear in plants (the hermaphrodite condition where both sexes appear on the same plant – see next section). Choose whichever method works the best for you, and fits within your time and space needs. The problem is that it won't completely eliminate the effect of male pollen. In some areas, male hemp plants, growing either naturally or on farms, may pollinate your plants. Pollen has been known to travel many miles from its source (traveling on birds, bees, or the wind) in search of female plants.

problem is solved. The disadvantage to waiting until the males show flowers at your site is that you may not notice them until they have already released their pollen. Although a female plant can continue to flower while it is producing seeds, only the healthiest ones will succeed at doing both.

Forced Flowering
Another method of growing only females is to screen them when they are very young—before the have been transplanted. This requires forcing them to flower at a young age by controlling their exposure to light but only works with mature plants that are capable of displaying sex.

When your seedlings have grown to about one foot in height they should be mature enough to begin the process of forced flowering. This means systematically depriving them of light for a minimum of 12 hours per

An easy to spot hermaphrodite with both male and female flower characteristics.

A well-watered grow will produce amazing plants like this.

Hermaphrodites

Marijuana, being a living organism driven to reproduce, may try to reproduce itself in spite of your efforts. In some cases female plants may grow male flowers thereby attempting to pollinate themselves or the plants nearby. Those plants bearing both male and female flowers are called hermaphrodites. Hermaphrodite plants that self pollinate tend to produce female and more hermaphrodites. Hermaphrodite plants are worth culling. If you must keep the hermaphrodite then picking off the male flower bunches can be one way of limiting the effect and preventing the crop from self pollinating. Hermaphrodites tend to occur naturally as a response to stress when plants are subjected to difficult conditions such as poor nutrients, excessive nitrogen, cold weather, or force flowering.

Watering Tips and Techniques

As mentioned before, watering needs depend on your growing site's location and the genetics of your crop. If you have a fairly humble-sized crop, then various hand-watering methods should suffice. Some growers haul water out to their site and then use watering pots or run hoses from a large container to their site. If you have been able to find

The Grow

a site that is fairly close to water, and you have a small number of plants, it may make the most sense to refill from the source and carry the water back and forth. This limits your liability since you'll never be questioned as to why you are bringing 100 gallons of water into the woods.

If you have a lot plants you may have to consider more elaborate methods, such as using battery- or gas-powered pumps. These have drawbacks in that they are usually very loud and the sound of a motor can carry for miles: not ideal for stealth operations. These systems require a source of power and constant water supply and sometimes need to be set up in an intricate way involving many subsections like tubing and platforms. Once in place, they have the ability to deliver tremendous volumes of water, according to the exact schedule that you need.

Another method is to fashion a slow-drip irrigation system. Using a one-gallon milk jug, poke a couple of pinholes into the bottom, which allows a steady, but small amount of water to be released. The advantage to this is that you only need refill the jugs, which, once in place, will water your plants on a consistent basis. The plant never suffers from too much watering as can happen if you travel to your site only occasionally. If your plants aren't

Watering Tips and Techniques

1. Always be careful when measuring the amount of fertilizer you'll be using to water your plants.

2. Put the fertilizer in the watering can, add water and make sure it all mixes up.

3. Slowly pour the water into the pot, making sure to water all of the soil thoroughly.

4. Make sure you don't get the fertilized water on the leaves of your plant because it could cause burn-damage.

getting enough water, then either add more jugs to water specific plants, or make the holes larger if the problem is the water retention abilities of the soil. Of course if you're just growing a few plants, and they are on your property, using an ordinary garden hose works great.

One very cheap and readily available source of water is of course, rainwater. Clean rainwater is a good source for your plants because tap water can contain unwanted chemicals. A lot of water systems use chemicals to clean the water to make it potable, or drinkable. They can also add additional chemicals to neutralize the taste, so that you don't taste the chemicals, just the water. Tap water pH may also be above or below 7. While this is great for humans and our finicky taste buds, it can be detrimental to the plants. One thing to watch out for is the amount of sodium (NaCl or salt) in the water.

Rainwater would be great for this garden because it would get between the hard-to-reach spots.

If you water your plants with overly salty water, their eventual size could be reduced by as much as 50%. Tap water can also contain chlorides, sulfates, and other solids, which helps to explain why the sales of water filtration systems are so brisk. It is also why using distilled water is recommended for young seedlings, before they are transplanted.

If you are concerned about the quality of water you are delivering to your plants (or drinking!) there are test kits available for sale at gardening and hardware stores. They will help you determine water quality and let you know which chemicals are prevalent in the largest amounts.

If you don't want to deal with this at all, then rainwater is an easy solution. The best way to catch rainwater is to place a large container under a drain spout during the rainiest months of the year. Usually this will happen in the spring so forethought is once again crucial to success. If the area being drained is generally clear of water-soluble chemicals, the rainwater should be perfect for the plants. Then your only problem is storing the water and transporting it to the site.

Pruning Your Plants

There are many reasons to prune a plant, but none of them are absolutely necessary to the health and survival

Good quality shears are essential for large-scale pruning. Hold them at a 45-degree angle to the shoot being cut.

There are many different ways to make your bud taste great. Nurture your outdoor grow and you'll have some California Orange fun in the sun with bud like this.

main branches and longer stems with large internodes (the space between two node regions) resulting in empty internode zones where plants have not produced any buds.

The prime outdoor growing months are July through August, so those will be the busiest in terms of both watering and pruning. The decision to prune is yours alone but there are certain issues to be aware of, including some things that should never be done.

Pruning Dos

In order to create smaller, denser plants, some growers will start pruning as soon as the plant reaches two feet in height. Using the thumb and forefinger, a grower should pinch off the tiny growing bud at the tip of the main branch or stem. The same thing can be done using either pruning shears or very sharp scissors. This forces the plant to branch outward, creating many strong branches able to produce large flowers. This is especially useful if you need to limit the height of your plants for any reason.

Smart growers will also prune if the plant is growing straight up with long empty spaces on which no branches are growing. Upward pruning forces the plant to focus its energy in a different direction, outward.

of the plant. If you do not prune, this will diminish neither the size nor the yield of your plants and pruning is not essential to growing high-quality marijuana, however some strains do respond well to pruning and sometimes do produce bigger yields so experimentation is advised.

Some of the reasons to prune are to reduce detection by limiting plant size, increase flower production, or simply have some (mostly) smokeable buds before the actual harvest time. Spacing is a key factor in the decision to prune since plants growing too close together will tend to shoot up in an attempt to reach the sunlight. This can lead to a lot of empty space on the

Hand Pruning

1. Pruning leaves by hand is a gentle and effective way to care for your growing cannabis plants. It is best to prune slowly and carefully, making sure to remove any dead, diseased, or damaged leaves, and any leaves that are blocking sunlight from the bud.

2. Simply pinch the stalk of the leaf between your thumb and forefinger and pinch it off, just as you would with your roses or tomatoes. This is the traditional method of pruning Cannabis Sativa and it has been done this way for centuries. And that resin on your hands afterwards? You guessed it. Hash.

Bubba Kush is an excellent strain by Dr. Greenthumb that grows great outdoors and offers a highly energetic and incredibly tasty smoke.

Pruning Don'ts

Pruning is not rocket science and ordinary growers use it to encourage growing patterns in plants all the time. However there are certain things that should be avoided.

Severe pruning done late in the season, in September for instance, will reduce yield since there will be less branches available to develop flowers and the plant will put its energy into leaf and branch development instead of flowering. Severe pruning is cutting a foot or more from the top of your plant or removing a long stem. The plant won't die, but since the yield has been drastically reduced you will feel the pain. Instead, practice consistent, small pruning measures to achieve the growing pattern you wish and prevent the need for such drastic measures later in the season.

Another thing to avoid is removing too many of the larger leaves, or fan leaves. Though they may appear to be limiting the sun that hits the bud sites because of the leaves surface area, these large leaves receive a ton of sunlight that is then converted into sugar and energy, which helps the plant to grow vigorously early in the season and to produce strong, full flowers late in the season.

Finally, when pruning, be sure to prune on sunny days as it allows the plant to heal with the sun acting

The Grow

Training

as a kind of disinfectant. Pruning imitates the effect that animals, or occasional insect predators, would have on the plant, which is why it can be considered natural and not such a bad thing. However, marijuana grown naturally without extenuating circumstances, like detection, will likely not need any pruning to be high yielding.

Training: An Alternative to Pruning

Another way to achieve the same end as pruning, without actually trimming your plants, is to tie or bend their branches to encourage outward growth. This process is called training.

One grower I knew needed a solution because he was growing on the small veranda outside of his apartment. A tall marijuana plant is easily recognized by both cops and ordinary passersby. Using string, he reined in what would have been easily a six or seven foot plant to a mere (and virtually undetectable) three feet in height. The plant stretched out almost the full length of his veranda. Come harvest time he found that this actually increased the yield, since new parts of the plant received strong doses of light. If you are considering this method, be sure to bend only the flexible part—the top six inches to a foot of the main stem.

1. Using string, tie a loose knot around the topmost part of the stem. Secure it by tying another knot closer to the ground. Gently pull the plant down as you go.

2. Training a plant to grow parallel with the ground exposes the main part of the stem to more sunlight, and can facilitate more bud producing branches.

Protecting Plants from Pests and Predators

One of the greatest advantages to growing plants outdoors is that your pest situation will be easier to deal with than it would be indoors. Indoors, your plants are the sole sustenance for insects and any infestation can spread incredibly rapidly. Outdoors, there will be insects in the soil, as well as those that thrive on green leaves in general, yet they should be kept in check by the ecosystem's natural way of maintaining balance.

Marijuana grows quickly and, though pests will damage plants, they will usually be repaired as the marijuana plant heals itself throughout its vegetative period. As far as pests are concerned, your plants will be at their most vulnerable in their infancy. This is when you might want to consider, should the occasion warrant, taking preventative measures.

During the first two months, as you are watering and paying attention to the myriad other problems that might be hindering growth, make sure that pests are kept under control. The insects that you'll want to pay the most attention to are slugs, snails, caterpillars, leaf-eating insects, and beetles. There are a few different means by which you can control these pests, using natural and artificial pesticides and repellents. Obviously, since you are going to be smoking these plants later, you want to pay special attention to the chemicals with which you treat them.

Natural Repellents
Companion Plants
Marijuana is a very hardy plant when grown outdoors with good nutrient-rich soil. Like most other plants, it produces natural toxins that serve as repellents to pests. Take advantage of this natural quality in other plants by using them as one natural way to help control your pest problem. Certain plants, especially mints, cabbages, and strong-smelling plants like onions, help repel a large range of assorted beetles and aphids. Onions can also help keep curious rabbits and deer away from your planting area. Geraniums or marigolds should also be considered for their ability to ward away leaf-eating insects as well as worms, beetles and other pests that bore into the stems or chew through the leaves of your plants.

Any choice you make should be planted very close to your crop, even

When you grow outdoors there are many pests that can feed on your plants.

interspersed with your plants as their natural insecticides only cover a very small area. At the same time, keep in mind that while companion plants should be planted close to your crops, you don't want them competing for water or nutrients.

When choosing a particular companion plant for its symbiotic qualities, make sure that you follow the proper growing instructions. Pay attention to what might normally grow in this area and choose those plants that have the best chance of surviving, diverting the feeding interests of the insects, and blending in better with the natural environment. Any information you need about companion plants, should be widely available either at a nursery or wherever you purchase seeds or transplants.

Using Predators as Deterrents

Another natural method that makes smart use of biology involves using predators such as ladybugs, praying mantises, or even lacewings. Their qualities of garden protection are widely known, and so it is possible to buy them commercially bred. The breeder should be able to tell you how they can be used most effectively and which insects they will eat. This information is useful once you know what type of insects to expect given your environment. Be aware though,

that buying insects won't work if your garden is small since there may not be enough food to support them.

Larger predators can also be used as means to protect your garden. If you are planting near a stream, it may be a good idea to encourage frogs, turtles, or lizards to frequent the area by leaving food there occasionally. Birds can also be persuaded to provide support, perhaps by leaving birdseed

These egg cases are great to hang in your plant. Once the mantids hatch, they'll consume all the aphids, beetles, flies, mosquitoes, and moths that can damage your grow. Great natural protection.

Protecting Plants from Pests and Predators

or even using a bird feeder.

Subtlety is probably best because you will want to draw the least amount of attention and suspicion. Casual observers might be drawn to your planting area if there are swarms of insects, reptiles, or birds in the area. This is one more instance in which respecting the natural environment will help keep your plants safe, and enable them to grow well.

Organic Insecticides

Thanks to the organic movement it is easy to find organic insecticides wherever nonorganic insecticides are found. Organic insecticides usually work by mimicking the natural pesticides produced by the plant, only in highly concentrated amounts. Pyrethrum is one of the most powerful and therefore most popular organic insecticides and is effective against a wide range of pests. Read the label carefully and make sure to follow the printed procedures, especially if the substance needs to be water-diluted.

The one drawback to organic insecticides is that even these may be indiscriminate killers, harming the insects and mammals that you might already be employing in your garden's defense. Unless your plants are truly being decimated, use any pesticide sparingly and with decreasing frequency as the plants mature,

Companion Planting

Geraniums.

Mint.

Marigolds.

Marigolds.

Ladybugs offer excellent natural protection for your outdoor grow.

preferably stopping after they have left the critical early period of life.

Soap and Water and Other Household Remedies

If even organic substances are a concern, using a mixture of about two tablespoons of soap diluted in one gallon of water provides an adequate level of protection. Spray the solution evenly over the entirety of the plant and let it sit for a few minutes, then wash the plants off thoroughly as soap may harm the leaves.

This is just one of many home remedies that growers employ. Investigate homeopathic gardening sites on the Web for other remedies. Some growers have told me that garlic washes can help repel beetles and that mixing rubbing alcohol with the soap and water formula can repel snails and slugs, however alcohol will remove wanted resin production. With anything you put on the plant though, be sure to find out exactly what you are spraying for, how long the solution should be applied for, and how thoroughly it should be diluted.

Protecting Against Rodents and Mammals

For pests that walk, run, or burrow, more extreme physical measures might need to be taken.

Grow organically and treat your plant right. You wouldn't want to flush all that work down the toilet.

Soap and Water

Thoroughly mix two teaspoons of dish detergent with one quart of water. Spray directly on plants and insects making sure to cover the bottom side of the leaves. Let the spray sit on the your plants for ten to twenty minutes, then completely rinse your plants to remove any remaining soap residue.

Garlic Water

1. Remove the skin from three or four cloves of garlic.

2. Mash the garlic with the flat side of a knife.

3. Boil one quart of water.

4. Steep the garlic in the water for about ten minutes.

5. Strain the water and pour into a spray bottle.

6. Mist your plants to deter soft-bodied insects.

Protecting Plants from Pests and Predators

Tobacco Water

1. Remove the dried tobacco from three cigarettes.

2. Insert the tobacco into a tea filter bag.

3. Pour one quart of boiling water over the tobacco stuffed teabag.

4. Steep in one quart of boiling water for approximately five minutes.

5. Strain the solids and pour the solution into a spray bottle.

6. Mist the leaves of your plants to deter soft-bodied insects.

This guy looks nuts, but no jokes, groundhogs and rabbits are known to eat the shoots and leaves of the cannabis plant, reducing a crop to nothing in a matter of days. You can keep them away by spreading predator urine around your grow.

Protecting Plants from Pests and Predators

Until the plant develops a hard stem, all manner of rodents, rabbits, and possibly even raccoons may decide to snack on your plants.

In Australia many growers experience problems with wombats and wallabies. Wombats are small and tend to burrow underground and eat at the roots, whereas wallabies will trample and eat the plants, as they do most leafy things they encounter.

Placing a hard object around the base of the plant, such as a coffee can with both ends removed, or anything else with similar hard shell properties, helps against most burrowing animals. Due to security concerns, most growers won't be able to erect chicken-wire enclosures, and the coffee can method is an alternative that is relatively easy, cheap, and less obvious however must be started early on or else it is harder to get the can around the stem without slicing it vertically.

Blood meal powder available at nurseries can be sprinkled around the perimeter to scare away rabbits and other animals that do most of their damage above ground, but may attract flesh-eating animals that will dig in search of flesh. Blood meal is also an organic food product so this must be factored in when feeding your plants. One way to solve both problems is to purchase urine from a predatory cat, like a puma or lion, and pour that around the perimeter instead of the blood powder. Deer, as well as the smaller mammals, won't go near the plants if they think they've stumbled across the path of a predator. This is another common item available over the Internet or in professional nurseries. If you can't get your hands on any big cat urine, human urine can ward off animals as well. We are, after all, one of the most destructive and predatory forces in nature.

When dealing with a possible pest problem, the first thing to do is to remain calm and not overreact. Before treating your plants or the area, inspect everything closely to determine exactly what type of infestation you might be experiencing. Unless the plant has begun to droop because a huge gash has been removed from its stalk, it can usually right itself as it matures. If the problem is cosmetic don't worry, as the plant will always be growing new leaves to catch the sun for photosynthesis.

Remember that some problems may simply be due to the local environment. For instance, other plants in the area may be the ones that are infested, and the insects are driven to your plants in search of new food sources. Find out what plants are around and which types of enemies they have, and then determine the best way to defend against them with minimal damage to your plants.

If all else fails and you must use a chemical insecticide, remember that they are not very specific in their killing and may harm beneficial insects and warm-blooded animals in the area. Remember as well that there is a potential threat to your health when you use chemicals, and your plants should only be harvested and smoked after the chemically active period is over. The manufacturer should make this information available, but always check these claims by conducting your own research as new studies seem to appear often contradicting previous information.

6

General Growing Tips

Sinsemilla is a term that we have all heard before, but what does it mean—besides really good smoke? It actually means seedless, literally without seed, from the Spanish sinsemilla, and refers to female marijuana plants grown to maturity without being fertilized by any male pollen. It is often not possible to ensure a sinsemilla crop when growing outdoors because wild male hemp seeds can pollinate your plants from as far as a mile away. Also, if you improperly sex your plants, or you wait too long to separate the males from the crop, then the risk of pollination could come from a plant within your growing site.

Sinsemilla

If you let your plants grow naturally and become pollinated, they will use their energy to produce more seeds than flowers since seeds are ultimately the key to reproduction. Within the seeds are all of the necessary materials needed to reproduce and create more plants. More seeds are good for the future of the plant, but not so good for the smoker. A sinsemilla plant will generally produce more resinous bud because none of the flowering area is consumed by seed.

In general, it is good idea to let your plants produce a few seeds especially if they are highly potent or tasty. If these seeds are properly labeled and stored you can selectively choose which plants you want to keep growing and avoid those that were not as sturdy or as desirable to reproduce in the next growing season. A plant that grows very tall, or produces strong, sweet-tasting buds, should be labeled and the seeds you recover from it after harvesting should receive special attention come the next spring. Another reason to let your females produce a few seeds is that it helps prevent the plant from becoming a hermaphrodite.

Seeding a Plant

In order to seed a plant, select a healthy male plant with well-branched, well-delineated stems and a rich green color. If at all possible, choose one that has grown quickly. Your goal is to capture the pollen from this male and control the process of pollination. One method is to prune the plant deeply, leaving only one branch that will bloom. The more male flowers that the plant produces, the more chance there is of random pollination, so stripping or pruning the other branches is a good way to play it safe.

Using a plastic bag that allows light to penetrate, cover the entire remaining portion of the plant and the remaining stem that is going to flower. Light is still important because decreased light makes pollen sacks develop more slowly. Once the male flower blooms, remove the pollinating flowers, and blow pollen on the females that you wish to seed. Do this before harvest because, like flowers, seeds require time to mature and should not be rushed. Another method, one that some growers favor because it is more exact, is to literally paint the pollen onto the female pistils.

A good indication of when to pollinate your females is when they appear white and fuzzy. Using the plastic bag in which the pollen was collected, cover the selected branches that you have pollinated for another day to ensure that the process was completed. Be very careful when removing the bag both from the male, as well as from the female when the process is completed. If this is done correctly, expect the seeds to be ready for harvesting in three to six weeks, when they begin to rattle in the pod.

Weather Extremes

Understanding the temperature ranges in your climate is most important at the beginning and end of the plant's life. Typically, if your climate is such that the start of the growing season, the beginning of spring, is marked by frosts, it may be necessary to begin growing in a greenhouse or controlled environment. A sudden change in the temperature most affects seedlings, killing them

This is a gorgeous outdoor medley of plants from CH9 Female Seeds featuring CH9 Jack, CH9 Flower, CH9 Mendocino, and CH9 Hashplant.

General Growing Tips

The benefit of growing in buckets is that you can move your plants whenever you want.

before they've had a chance to develop resiliency. As the plants mature, they grow thick stems that shield them from the effects of the weather.

You may choose to start your plants indoors and transplant them later, so that they can receive the full benefit of growing outdoors in the natural sunlight, but reach maturity well before the weather changes. Forcing plants to harvest can be tricky, but might be achieved by controlling the light the plants receive. Covering them with something heavy and opaque would be the best option, but is an imperfect solution. Black polyethylene film, dark plastic bags or even large cardboard or packaging can be used to provide the uninterrupted darkness required. Other solutions for growers in these areas would be to plant in containers. This gives you the option of starting early, moving the plants outside when the sun is strong, and moving them into dark areas in order to induce flowering.

At the other end of the marijuana plant's life cycle, some regions will experience frost even before the first days of fall. Though the plant can withstand some frosting, repeated exposure to the cold weather or frequent frost episodes might cause the plants to lose both potency and taste. If they are not harvested quickly then the entire crop could

This wall of corn not only protects the grow from prying eyes, but also provides a great wind break for your plants.

General Growing Tips

be lost. Watch the sun, and consult nurseries and resources for growers of perennials that begin in the spring such as tomatoes and corn. This should give you a sense of when frosts usually occur and when the plants should be harvested. Once you have been through a couple of harvests, you'll know exactly when the time is right. The margin for error in timing is greater in the fall, certainly, than in the spring.

If there are no heavy freezes in your area, it might be possible to grow year round. The plants will generally not be that tall, but will bud very well as long as the soil and water are sufficient, and the light they receive is good. The winter sun is not as strong but it is adequate to fuel plant growth. Once you've reached springtime, simply trim the plants and the long days will retrigger the growth stage for the natural harvest time in fall.

Wind Protection

In windy areas it is a good idea to plant crops on the perimeter of your growing area closely together to serve as a windbreak to protect the other plants. Tying plants to stakes driven into the ground, or constructing a rope and stick fence, are two ways you might achieve this. The drawback of course, is that those plants will be competing with each other very intensely for soil nutrients, sunlight, and water. Another method you could use to deal with windy areas is to keep your plants clipped. This will likely limit your harvest slightly, but the plants will also adapt and become denser in their branching, hence their flowering.

A tasty Indica Iranian Auto Flower from Dr. Greenthumb Seeds that has a very fast outdoor finishing time.

Chapter 6

When you bring all factors together you end up with beautiful plants like this.

Stress as a Means for Increasing Plant Vigor

Usually, stress inhibits the growth of the plant, or will damage the yield at the time of harvest. Intentionally underwatering around harvest is a kind of stress that growers will use to improve on the bud quantity. Although it is wise to limit the water plants receive as you reach the harvest time, be careful not to let the plants get so dry that they wilt or burn in the sunlight. As the leaves drop off, or turn brown, the flowers that remain might resemble the resin in color and harshness of smoke.

Some stresses produce far more dramatic results and are based on less credible cultivation sense. These include: splitting the base of the plant with nails, severe pruning, and bending or contorting the stem. The goal of these actions is to increase the bud quantity of the marijuana plant. Although there does appear to be a relationship between stress and bud quantity however the fundamentals of the growing process are most important. Choice of location, soil and its nutrient content, and using good seeds are far more important to yield and potency than the stresses placed upon a plant.

Second Harvest

There are a couple of techniques that growers employ as they near harvest time that can lead to what is known as

General Growing Tips

a second harvest. This will obviously depend on the climate in your area, as crops grown in northern climes may be vulnerable to frost or other adverse affects of seasonal change. For temperate zones and areas in which the weather in the beginning of fall is relatively benign, it may be possible to initially harvest your plants in a manner that will enable you to harvest a second time, a few weeks later.

The process starts with the initial harvest. After you've taken the bulk of the harvest, leaving only the very smallest flowers, and most of the leaf, you should repeat the process that initially started your growth cycle. Water your plants thoroughly, and mix in a freshly prepared batch of fertilizer to supply your plants with all the necessary materials for growth. The goal is to encourage the plants to return to the start of flowering and to continue flowering. Leaving the leaves encourages new flower growth since they will still be receiving and processing copious amounts of sunlight.

The fact that the light will have changed means that the plant will naturally be in the flowering stage. However, if your climate stays relatively mild, or even if you are in tropical areas, then it is likely that you could continue the vegetative state for longer by breaking up the period of light. To do

If you put companion plants near your grow, you'll not only be able to fend off some pests, but bring in beneficial insects.

this, shine a bright flashlight over the entire surface area of the plant, during the night. This will, as mentioned before, encourage growth. Once you are ready for the plants to flower, stop the interrupted darkness. Since it takes a few weeks to flower, factor this in when deciding how long to enable growth. If the frost of cold weather is coming in two weeks, you should have encouraged flowering at least three weeks before.

Harvesting, Curing, and Storage

Finally, after months of preparation, work, and careful maintenance, the time to harvest will arrive. Harvesting is not as easy a task as just cutting down your plants, waiting a week or so for them to dry, and then getting as high as a kite. There are still signs to watch for and critical mistakes to avoid, or you risk nullifying all of your hard work over the preceding months. The most important of these is getting the timing right.

The Big Payoff

Watching the weather and paying close attention to your plants will let you know when they are ready for harvest. After a certain point, the potency of marijuana plants will begin to degrade from its peak point. But harvesting too soon can be worse in terms of reducing the potential potency/yield of your plants. Balancing this means understanding the rhythm of the blooming period that your plants will undergo. If in doubt, it is best to err on the side of patience.

Throughout the flowering period, the end stage of your crop's development, the sun's strength in conjunction with the changing seasons should be your guide. The plant, through its changing appearance, will also send signals that clearly identify when the right time has arrived. Keep an eye on the weather since the conditions on the day you actually cut the plants is very important.

Follow the Sun

There is a primitive element to growing outdoors in that you return to the simplest of all means to measure time: the sun. The amount of light your crop has been receiving has been the engine of growth throughout the long growing season. As the summer ends, it is important to watch the sun and monitor again how much light your plants are receiving.

At most elevations your plants will receive upwards of 14 hours of light during the peak midsummer growing season. As August turns into September, the amount of sunlight drops considerably. In the month of September alone we lose about 90 minutes of sunlight. Plants sense this change and the increasing darkness sends a signal that starts flowering in mature plants.

Recall that during the sex selection process varying the light had the effect of forcing mature plants to bloom. This is precisely what nature does as the rotation of the earth reduces the hours of daylight. Once this dips below 12 or 13 hours it is only a matter of days until blooming occurs with mature plants. The mechanism in

The darkness this area gets when the sun goes down will signal nighttime to the plants.

plants that determines day from night is very sensitive and can be influenced by artificial lights. That is why growing areas must not be situated near street or other electrical lighting. Night must mean darkness, which is what happens naturally as the seasons change. It is therefore necessary to grow in an environment in which the changing of the seasons is well differentiated. Believe me, if you decide to grow, fall will become your favorite season.

From Bloom to Bud

The autumnal equinox usually marks the point at which you should begin to consider harvesting your plants, but this is not a hard and fast rule. Stop watering a few weeks prior to the equinox and, as the date approaches, pay attention to the signals your plants are sending you. At this stage in the plant's maturity upward growth stops and it shifts its energy into flowering. There are two things to pay attention to during this time: the rate at which the plant flowers and the plant's physical characteristics.

The blooming period of your plants should be your number one concern in choosing the right time to harvest. Once the light has dipped and flower production has started, expect your plants to bloom between six and twelve weeks. Much like popping popcorn, the flowers will appear slowly

Harvesting, Curing, and Storage

at first, and then arrive with increasing frequency. With each visit you'll notice both the new flower production as well as growth in the ones that have already bloomed. The bloom ends when new flower production declines markedly.

About a week after the bloom has ended, the plants will have achieved their maximum growth and this is the right time to harvest. When you are making popcorn you are supposed watch for the increased time in between pops. If you leave it on too long, you run the risk of burning the already popped kernels. As is the case sometimes, there may be more kernels that could be popped, but leaving it in the oven is too great a risk. A similar idea is at work in flower production. Even though the plant may be able to produce a few more flowers, waiting to harvest can be detrimental to the overall yield. Waiting for a few more, at the expense of weakening the existing ones, is not worth it.

Another sign that you're ready to harvest will be apparent all over

This strain of kush would make a great smoke for anyone wanting to relax.

Romulan is an Indica strain that is known for its potency and therapeutic qualities.

This plant is almost ready for harvest. Very soon, the pistils will start to change color and it will be ready for harvest.

the plant in the leaves and the buds themselves. The physical characteristics of the plant will change considerably. The larger leaves will turn a yellow-brown color which tells you that the plant is dying. The stigmas of mature plants will wither at the base of the buds, while remaining a healthy white color on top.

Another sign, and one in which there is a bit of latitude, is in the color of the buds themselves. It is a good idea to pick them at the first sign that they are losing their rich green color. If they turn brown, a sign that they've withered a bit, the buds will smoke more harshly. The one benefit to waiting until you near this point is that the resin glands will contain more resin, and some people don't mind the harsher smoke since they bargain that they are receiving a stronger, more intense high. This is a personal decision and one that you'll learn more about over your successive harvests.

The changing hours of the sunlight are of course the most important aspect of your plants' lives. Plants are naturally in tune to the changing amounts of light and darkness that they are receiving, and the increasingly longer hours of darkness sends a signal to a plant that it must mature. Depending on where you grew your plants, and whether or not they were started indoors and then replanted,

Harvesting, Curing, and Storage

the sun will be the most important predictor in knowing that harvest is approaching. Some growers, like those in many parts of Australia, Hawaii, and the southern parts of North America, can often get two or more harvests a year, because the sun provides plenty of light throughout the year. In that case, the plants will grow large, flower as if to reproduce naturally and then begin again. But since they are already quite large, and have plenty of leaves to catch the sunlight, the second harvest occurs in much less time than did the first.

For the rest of us though, growers in areas in which it is important to have your plants removed by the end of summer and the onset of the first frost, the sun is a lifeline to our finished product. The middle of the summer, which in the Northern Hemisphere falls on the 21st of June, has as much as 15 hours of sunshine. Marijuana plants will not typically flower unless they receive at least 12 hours of darkness a day. Indoor growers are typically able

These well-trimmed buds will be ready to harvest in days.

The steaks will provide support as these plants grow to their full potential.

to harvest more often because they control the light. The trade-off for the outdoor grower is receiving more in less frequent harvests. If you only have a few plants, it is sometimes possible to cover them completely and induce harvesting, but this is not a functional reality for most growers.

The light and darkness factor works both ways though. Some growers will actually shine very bright lights, like halogens, on their plants during the night in order to reset the internal clock. This is useful if you wish your plant to grow in size and not begin its flowering. In Australia some Sativa varieties can grow to 16 feet with internodes around 3 to 4 inches in variety. Obviously a plant of that size will produce a large amount of recoverable crop, but getting it that size requires a year-round growing season. To get it that size they may need to convince the plant that it is not quite time to flower, and that perhaps it should continue using its energy toward leaf production and upward reaching.

Harvesting Your Plants

The process of harvesting is very simple and there are several methods that you can choose from. The goal is to get the plants out of the ground, so use any method that will accomplish that goal. As we have discussed, the timing of the harvest is the issue that most growers

Harvesting, Curing, and Storage

have problems with, since they don't quite know when their plants are done.

The legal issues concerning your plants are at their height during the harvest. It is hard to deny ownership of the plants as you are cutting them down. Take extra precautions as the date approaches. Tell nobody that the harvest date is approaching and on the day you're actually going to the fields be extra evasive about your whereabouts. Every time you visit your plants, from planting through to harvesting, you should always make sure the area is clear. On the harvest day or days, don't let your excitement about the forthcoming yield cause you to lower your guard. Take the proper steps and plan your trip well. Decide how you're going to harvest and bring the appropriate tools. Bring bags that aren't see-through and cut the plants into manageable lengths. Aesthetically it is preferable to see the long stalks almost as they were in the ground, but this is usually not practical. Working quickly and efficiently, cut the stalks into sizes that will fit in your bags. At the time of your harvest and during the drive home, your legal risk is at its highest. You will be in possession of a large amount of marijuana.

Use the methods described above to decide when to harvest and simply get the plants out of the ground. Any harvesting should be done well before the first frost, and ideally in good, clear, sunny weather. If, for whatever reason, you harvest in the rain, don't worry; drying times won't be increased too much, and both the flowers and the resin glands will be fine. Once you're safely home with your plants secured, relax, you're almost there.

Great Expectations: Predicting Yield

There are no hard and fast rules to predicting yield but there are indications as to whether it will be a great, good, or disappointing growing season. Soil quality, water, and of course sunlight are all variables, which if you account for them, will enhance rather than hinder your harvest. As a minimum five-foot tall plant should produce around two to six ounces of recoverable bud. As the plant grows taller and bushier you can expect more. However, any changes that have occurred since the plant has reached harvest time such as pest infestation, or even fungus, etc... will severely limit your yield.

Before you harvest make sure to flush the plant with plain water.

These buds have been hung up in a well-ventilated space to dry out.

Drying Your Bud

Once the plants have been harvested, they have obviously ceased to produce new cannabinoids and resins. The main changes to the potency will be negative, but effective drying and storage can help mitigate the effects. Most of the weight contained in the plant is water and drying will cause the liquid to evaporate, ensuring that the buds will burn evenly and smoke well. If you were impatient, and tried to quickly cut, dry, and smoke a bud prior to your harvest, you probably noticed how poorly it smoked. This is due to the water that comprises well over half (more that 60%) of its weight. It probably didn't get you high either, since drying also helps to activate the cannabinoids within the plant. But since you are a prudent grower, you waited until your buds were perfectly ripe and ready.

There are several methods to consider when drying, and they range from quick and easy, to slightly more involved but not much more difficult. The first method that I will describe is the slowest but by the far the most effective in terms of sealing in the aroma and taste of your buds. Simply hang the buds upside down in a secure dark place such as a closet or room with sealed windows and a good draft. It is important that air be able to circulate while the plants are being dried. This

means that you may have to exercise some caution in terms of where you might be able to safely dry the plants— they will be very, very pungent.

Use a fan to keep the air circulating and be sure to separate the plants or you could lose a lot of

your buds to mold. Removing the large green leaves and stems speeds the drying process since those parts of the plant contain much more water. Do not dry the plants in the sunlight as the buds will lose potency, their color and some of their taste. They may also

These buds are almost fully dried.

Leave some space between buds to ensure no mold appears.

become brittle, which will make them smoke very harshly.

If your drying room is very humid, or if it is raining outside, pay special attention to your bud and make sure that the room is well ventilated. You will have to be especially vigilant under these conditions with respect to mold. This is the reason that the drying area should be secure: your multiple trips should not arouse suspicion. Expect the drying time for a large amount of plants to be at least ten days to two weeks.

A quicker method for drying plants that may be more convenient for some growers is to separate and suspend them as before, but increase the temperature in the room to more than 90° Fahrenheit (about 32° Celsius). This will probably require an electric- or gas-powered heater. The room should again be well ventilated, but if the buds are rather tightly packed a large amount can be dried in less than a week. If there is no specific need to do this, then taking the extra week is worth it. For one thing, if buds are dried close together and any mold should appear, its spread will be rapid and fatal. Also, the increased heat can cause the plants to dry unevenly depending on their orientation in the room. Finally, they might dry out too quickly and once again you'll face the problem of dry, brittle buds that don't smoke evenly or taste nearly as

This box of dried, manicured bud is just dying to be smoked.

good as naturally grown buds should taste. Pay attention and make the necessary adjustments. If the room is too humid increase the airflow without decreasing the temperature. Make sure that heat is reaching all parts of the plant equally and your buds should be fine. The best method however is to allow the buds to dry in a cool dark place over the course of a few weeks. Patience is a virtue in terms of well cured bud.

If you want to quick dry just a few buds for more immediate consumption, place then on a cookie sheet or oven tray, and bake at a temperature of between 150 and 200° Fahrenheit (about 65 to 95° Celsius) for about 10 minutes. It won't taste as good as the slow-cured bud and will likely be harsh, as all water has been aggressively removed from the plant and plant chlorophyll has not degraded, but you shouldn't sacrifice any of the bud's potency. Watch it carefully, though; if it burns or becomes too dry you might as well add it to your organic compost heap for next year's crop because it won't be any good for smoking. This would only happen if you're careless, or if the heat is well above 200° Fahrenheit. This extreme measure is best used as a short-term remedy to test the quality of the pot,

Cup full of goodness.

or perhaps to tide you over through a dry spell while you're waiting the week or so for the main harvest. Whichever method you choose, make sure that you monitor each bud for signs of mold and remove those immediately from the drying area. Mold can be as detrimental to your plant as any other pest, human or animal.

Curing Your Harvest

Some growers recommend curing, but there is really no need, and it will change the flavor of the pot. Improper curing will result in THC decay and will also likely change the color of your bud to a dark brown tint that resembles old or dehydrated marijuana. You've probably never smoked cured marijuana so there is really no need to start now, and, in any event, it is one more delay before you may begin smoking your harvest. When done correctly, curing can enable the pot to smoke much more smoothly and reduce the minty taste that may accompany fresh outdoor grown pot. Most of the techniques used to cure marijuana are adapted from tobacco curing, so if you are considering curing I would recommend buying a book that treats the matter in depth and using that as a reference. Most growers are more than satisfied with smoking their own naturally grown, uncured bud.

Store your bud carefully.

Storage

The best way to store your marijuana for long periods of time is in airtight glass containers in the freezer. A very cold refrigerator compartment would work as well as a freezer, but safety concerns might dictate that you avoid such a public place as your kitchen for storage.

Light will degrade the THC and plastic bags can leak. Plastic containers and tins can work fine for a few weeks but should not be relied upon for long-term storage. Over time, the THC of pot stored in unsealed containers begins to degrade resulting in a very poor high. There is also a danger of the buds drying out and losing their freshness.

Large buds, dried adequately and packaged into an airtight container, without too much exposure to light, will remain just as fresh as the first day you stored them for at least a year or more. By that point you'll need those containers for the fresh crop of goodness that you'll be about to harvest.

8

Advanced Growing Tips

There are many reasons to clone, but nearly all of them involve wanting to continue a special plant from a special strain. The other big reason, which amounts to the same thing, is for seed production. After a successful harvest a grower might fall in love with a particular strain and want to always have some more of it in successive harvests. Though at first blush it sounds difficult, and maybe even a little bit unethical, rest assured it's easier than you think and as old as cultivation itself. Many people have cloned already by taking cuttings from non-marijuana.

Cloning

There are many reasons to clone, but nearly all of them involve wanting to continue a special plant from a special strain. The other big reason, which amounts to the same thing, is for seed production. After a successful harvest a grower might fall in love with a particular strain and want to always have some more of it in successive harvests. Though at first blush it sounds difficult, and maybe even a little bit unethical, rest assured it's easier than you think and as old as cultivation itself. Many people have cloned already by taking cuttings from non-marijuana plants, letting them root, and repotting them. The principle is the same with marijuana, but there are a few extra steps you may want to try to ensure success, since this is not just an ordinary houseplant.

Though almost any mature plant can be cloned, it is probably best to choose a younger one that is about two to three months old. If it is unavoidable, and you have to use an older plant, then the process doesn't change, but be more attentive to the needs of the plant, especially its watering needs, in the first few weeks. Before you clip a branch from the parent plant, heavily water the plant and check the pH of the soil. Know what is within good range for your climate and soil type. If necessary, you may need to make adjustments before proceeding. Heavily water the plant for about three days.

When clipping the branch, try to choose one of the larger ones near the bottom with good, full leaves. Cut at an angle, as you would flowers before placing them in a vase. As soon as you've cut the branch place it in some lukewarm water. After transporting the cutting back to your nursery (or greenhouse) prepare it for rooting in small peat pots or rooting cubes, which are available at any plant store. They will also offer soil-less mixtures for rooting cuttings. These are usually gel mixtures or liquids that are diluted in mineral water or other not-tap water. Some

This OG Kush from Dr. Greenthumb has dense resinous buds and a spicy, lemon taste.

growers prefer rolling the branch in a rooting powder or gel. Each method has its adherents and detractors. Decide for yourself over time.

Keep the cuttings moist by periodically spraying them with water and place them in an enclosure that allows airflow but keeps them from getting too dry. One idea a grower in San Francisco uses is a tent made out of resealable freezer bags. This allows him to leave a small portion open to allow air to circulate throughout the day; easy access for the multiple water mistings the clones receive per day; and a tent to trap the humidity inside. At the same time, expose the plants to near constant light—much more than 12 hours a day—unless you are cloning for sex. In a few weeks, the clones should develop roots. Replant carefully.

Cloning for Sex

When cloning for females however, there is one extra step you should take and that is to sex the little cuttings. Instead of exposing the plants to near constant light you have to actually convince them that they are flowering by depriving them of light. The cuttings must also be mature enough to flower and thus taken from plants that have about three to four weeks vegetative growth in them which is distinguished by calyx development. For about two weeks make sure the plants receive complete darkness for at least 12 hours straight. If you make a mistake and some light, even the smallest amount gets to them, then you can't count the days leading up to that and you have to start over.

If you've done your job correctly, after two weeks tiny blossoms will have appeared in the node region of your cuttings. Keep flowering them and eventually it will be clear which are female and which are male. Transplant the females and get rid of the males unless you want them for seeding or something. Your plants will return to the vegetative state in a little less than a week provided that they receive at least 13 hours of sunlight but more light is better. If this does not work then bathe them in light for 24 hours for at least 2 days before letting them re-sync with the seasonal light pattern.

Testing During Harvesting

In addition to what was stated under harvesting in chapter 7, there are slightly more methodical ways to determine when to harvest your grow, and how well you do this can impact both potency and yield. The first harvest will be a learning experience rife with miscalculations and potentially damaging errors. Pay attention to the decisions you make and the steps you take. As long as you don't do things in a haphazard way, you

Margoot from Green Devil Genetics is a delicious and powerful Sativa/Indica strain that boasts great THC percentages and heavy resin production.

should be able to make tremendous gains in quality on successive harvests, until you get a strong feel for when the plants are ready to be cut.

Choosing the plant that has matured the most rapidly, take several samples every day. The size of these samples should be relatively small: enough to get high once or twice. In between, you might want to smoke other types of marijuana to compare the potency and taste of what is currently growing.

Each time you sample your grow, try to choose flowers that come from the same position on the plant, and

that are similar in appearance, smell, and size, since this will give you some consistency. While this method would not hold up to rigorous scientific scrutiny, as the other plants in your garden grow to the same height and display the same characteristics, you'll have an idea of how they will smoke and the kind of high they will produce. This sort of testing, in combination with the visual cues mentioned in the section on harvesting—the appearance of full flowers and resinous plants—will help you to ensure that each successive harvest will be better than the last.

Chapter 8

Outdoor Cloning

1. Simple organic pots.

2. Rapid rooter disks provide nutrients.

3. Insert disks into base of grow cups.

4. Clones should be taken from a healthy plant.

5. Use sharp scissors or a razor blade and cut diagonally.

6. Scrape off outer layer of stem to encourage new root growth.

7. Dip cuttings in rooting compound.

8. Place stem in the disk medium.

9. Water or mist frequently.

Emergency Plant Fixes

As a grower, the ability to spot sick plants and diagnose their ailments will be of great importance to you. This is particularly so with marijuana, since the one thing you normally cannot do is ask for external help. This section will help you to recognize deficiencies in your plants and diagnose and remedy the situation.

Remember that it is possible for your plants to have too much of a good thing, as well as not enough of the things that they need most. The first step is to think about how balanced your plants' diet has been (N-P-K) and then check the pH of both the soil and the water that you're feeding to them. If those both check out but your plants are still showing signs of distress, then your problem may be sunlight, since you can control the pH and the nutrient regimen. On the other hand, if your plant is ailing, sunlight is plentiful and the water you're feeding it is okay, then you have nutrient issues.

Nutrient Deficiencies

The most basic problems with your plants will be that certain nutrients are unable to be absorbed by the roots, or are not extant in the soil itself. Soil amendments are great in this situation because they provide the nutrients that a plant needs; however, recognizing which nutrient is not being

Is this bud ready to harvest? Take a small sample and smoke-test it to see.

Not all grows look as good as this one. If your plants look sick, you need to test the pH of the soil and the water you are giving them.

absorbed may be difficult. There are signs to look for, but even these may not suffice since certain deficiencies will produce similar symptoms. The following are some helpful hints for detecting which nutrient may be deficient in your plants' diet.

Nitrogen (N) plays a very big role in the life of your plants. It is responsible for production of chlorophyll—photosynthesis—and also amino acids, which are the building blocks of proteins. Nitrogen deficiencies usually start on the lower to middle part of the plant and mostly affect older leaves. Plants that exhibit nitrogen deficiencies tend to be green on top, but the leaves yellow toward the bottom. This is especially common once your plants have begun to flower since the plant is utilizing its cache of nutrients stored in its leaves. If your plant is in the vegetative growth stage then this is a problem since the yellow leaves are no longer aiding in harnessing the power of the sun to grow.

There are a few ways to rapidly increase your plant's intake of nitrogen. One of them is to use blood meal. Other sources of nitrogen are dried blood, cottonseed meal, bat guano (or bat excrement), fish meal (or fish emulsion), as well as worm castings (again, excrement). All of these are available at any good gardening store and definitely online. There are also

The brown, dull color at the edge of this cannabis plant's leaves could mean that it is suffering from a phosphorus deficiency.

Jack Fem from CH9 Female Seeds is a great all-around plant that offers a long-lasting high.

chemical amendments that are quite easy to find at any store, for example, Miracle-Gro or other brand-name plant foods. Nitrogen deficient plants usually recover in about a week, but sadly, the affected leaves will never recover. They will drop off, but new ones will replace them. It is important to always check the pH before and after adding soil amendments since some of them will cause fluctuations in your pH.

Phosphorus (P) is beneficial to your plants in many ways. It aids in root growth and strengthens the leaves and stems. It is also very influential during flowering as it helps to germinate seedlings. It is typically needed in large amounts, and most soils that are N-P-K balanced will include heavy doses.

Phosphorus deficiencies cause the plant to seem weak and lifeless and will slow the plant growth. The edges of your plant's leaves will be brown or very dull in color and curl inwards. Some growers have noticed that whenever the temperature is cold, usually early or late in the season, their plants have a hard time absorbing the phosphorus in the soil, which calls for a larger infusion than usual. Other factors that contribute to phosphorus deficiencies include cold, wet soil or very alkaline soil.

Any organic or store-bought fertilizers or plant foods that have phosphorus in them will fix a

This bud is in flower and should be ready to harvest soon.

phosphorus deficiency. Make sure though that the N-P-K ratio is above five. Some all-purpose plant foods, such as Miracle-Gro, will also work— although make sure that you blend at half the recommended amount since too much may be toxic to your plants. Bonemeal is another good source of phosphorous, as are the castings of bats and worms. Another suggestion, if you can find it, is crab shell or crab meal, which some growers swear by as

an all-purpose fixer, but especially for phosphorus deficiencies.

Potassium (K), the last of the major soil nutrients, plays a big role as well. This nutrient helps your plants with disease resistance and water respiration, and assists the leaves in their photosynthesis production and conversion. Potassium also helps to circulate water throughout the entire body of the plant and is necessary during both the vegetative growth and

Keep your eye on the pH level of the water you give your plants. Do it right and you'll end up with some very nice buds.

flowering stages.

Having too little potassium in your cannabis plants may cause their leaves to grow very slowly and seem to be scorched around the tips and edges. Your plants may bend too easily and become broken by the wind. The more mature leaves may show different patches of color (mottle) and turn yellow between the veins, followed by entire leaves that turn dark yellow and die. The plant's overall growth slows down and finally, and most damaging, your flowering will be delayed.

Potassium deficiencies are relatively easy to fix because this nutrient is absorbed by your plants very quickly and easily under a variety of pH conditions. If you are using store-bought fertilizers, simply adding some that contains potassium should solve your problem relatively easily. Some organic fixes include: wood ashes, kelp meal, granite dust, or sulfate of potash.

This list is by no means exhaustive, but many of the problems you encounter with your plants will be nutrient-related and if your soil has these three basic elements, your plants should be healthy enough to harvest. A more complete list of additives is given in the soil section of chapter 3. With most of these solutions, you'll see results about a week after adding the amendments.

Advanced Growing Tips

Early detection is always the key.

One quick note about diagnosis: since some of the deficiencies are very similar to one another a good idea might be to flush the soil with water before adding anything. Sometimes your deficiency is actually caused by having too much of a nutrient. For instance, having too much potassium can prevent the absorption of iron. Always flush, then pH test, add, then test again. Another reason to test the pH is because almost anything added is best absorbed when the pH level is as close to seven as possible. The best way to add any nutrient is to foliar feed the plant by making a tea and spraying the leaves. Never do this at the hottest part of day. Either early in the morning or just after the sun sets are the best times.

Pest Problems

If you find you're having excessive pest problems, where whole leaves are being completely chewed away or your branches and stems are being bored into, a quick and useful solution is to mix up a combination of liquid soap and water and spray the plant. Another pesticide that growers use is a combination of tobacco and water. Unroll a cigarette and let it sit in water for three or four days. Then pour the solution into a spray bottle and administer it to your plants. The

These are some of the biggest roots I've ever seen on a cannabis plant. Protect them from root rot by adding a few tablespoons of hydrogen peroxide to your water.

problem with using commonly sold pesticides is that eventually you're going to smoke this plant and, by extension, those same chemicals.

This guide should help you ascertain what is going on with your plants, but it is not indicative of all that might go wrong with your plants. Your number one concern should be keeping the pH balanced appropriately, since this will aid in the proper uptake of all the nutrients that a plant needs in both its vegetative and flowering states.

Advanced Water Remedies

There are myriad things that can go wrong when growing cannabis but most of the ones that you control

Epsom salts can be used to treat the nutrient deficiency in the soil around your plant.

revolve around pH levels. Your eyes are the first line of defence as you'll be able to see problems ranging from misshapen or damaged leaves to fungus, but there are things that you can't see. It is therefore a very good idea to get a pH tester that enables you to check both soil and water. Electronic ones with digital displays are of course easier to use, but also more expensive. At any good home improvement or gardening store you'll also be able to find liquid pH testers,

and these do a good job as well and are not as expensive but may be a bit more complicated to use. In a pinch, or if you are on a budget, pH strips will work, but they cannot be completely trusted. If you find your readings are not jibing with what the plant or soil looks like then the tester may be the problem. Sometimes, however, the soil readings may consistently be in a good range (between 6.5 and 8.5), your soil composition may be sound (whether you are using an organic mix

or chemical solution) but there are still problems with the plant. In these cases the problem is likely the water. Often it's the pH of the water, but other times it may be as simple as over- or underwatering the plants.

Overwatering is a serious mistake that is very common among new growers because the assumption is that since water is needed, too much of a good thing can't be bad. The problem is that too much water deprives the roots of oxygen and so they slowly die. A quick and easy sign of overwatering is that the plant will droop and seem as if it is changing colors, the green luster turning yellow. Leaves will fall off the plant and eventually even leaves that look healthy will die and fall. Another problem that comes from too much water is that it can leech vital nutrients from the soil before the plants have had a chance to absorb them.

The easiest way to prevent overwatering is to check the soil before you water. Insert a ruler a few inches into the soil and if it comes out dry and with no soil adhering, then it's time to water. Unless you are growing in a very arid environment, your plants will only need a good water twice or so a week. The reason for this is that the topsoil is not indicative of the moistness of the rest of the soil. If you are using an irrigation system, then you'll have to adjust either the flow of the water, or

Advanced Growing Tips

A Nutritional Herbal Tea for your Marijuana Garden

1. Ingredients: one tablespoon each of comfrey, alfalfa, and nettle leaves.

2. Place ingredients in a glass container.

3. Pour one quart of boiling water over the leaves.

4. Steep for ten minutes, then cool to room temperature.

5. Strain the liquid and discard the leaves.

6. Pour the tea directly into the soil or mist on leaves of your plants.

This transplant is moving into a healthy vegetative stage.

the distance of the spouts from the plant. This problem is unlikely to occur if your plants are in the ground since excess water will be absorbed by the surrounding soil, but if your plants are in pots, this could be a serious issue because they could develop root rot.

Root rot is what happens to roots deprived of oxygen, and it could kill your plant. A slightly involved way to control water is to add a small amount (a few tablespoons) of hydrogen peroxide to your water. This works because the chemical compound is comprised of oxygen, but it also has an added benefit: it will kill any bacteria in your soil arising as a result of the rot. But if this doesn't work, your alternatives (searching for the roots that are affected, killing them, then transplanting to a larger pot; or cutting the plant down) aren't very good. **Underwatering** is another serious problem and its effects will look similar, with the exception that the leaves falling off will be shrivelled and decimated. The plant is literally dying of thirst and, as it starts to wither, it is using all the available resources on subsistence and so will let the leaves, the extensions, go. This means that during this period of its vegetative state, the plant will stop producing new branches and leaves. Even though you can correct the problem quite simply (add water) the effects may continue to be felt at harvest when your plants may be smaller and their smoke may be more harsh than expected.

Typically, any other problems having to do with water will be related to pH. The problem will go something like this: the soil has a nutrient deficiency, so you attempt to remedy the situation by doing something like adding Epsom salts or worm castings, or you mix in a balanced organic nutrient mix with your watering regimen. After about a week, the soil pH levels begin to rise (soil is less acidic) but the plant's problem is still apparent. Concerned, you add more nutrients either directly to the soil, or in a tea and the problem only seems to get worse, (the pH drops). In cases like this, it is probably the water that is the problem, and so, before you completely lose your mind, be sure to test the water. Most major municipalities chlorinate their water to kill bacteria harmful to humans. This water should never be used when you are germinating or flowering your plants, and if you must use it when your plants are in the vegetative growth stage, you should let it sit for at least twenty-four to forty-eight hours so that the chlorine can evaporate. Chlorine is very acidic and, once added, it can lower the pH levels in the soil, preventing the absorption of whatever nutrient or supplement you are trying to add.

Nutrient Disorders /Fertilizer Corrections

If your plants are showing signs of distress such as drooping, mottling of the leaves, or loss of large amounts of leaves, then a fix of some sort is needed. Remember what your soil composition is and how much water you've given them. If your soil is too acidic or too alkaline, you'll need to stabilize the plant and return the soil to balance. Usually adding an organic supplement will help swing the soil back in the direction you need. Remember that some supplements work more quickly than others and choose based on timing (point in the growing season) and urgency (how bad your plants look). If it is later in the season, then a quick-acting organic additive applied with a spray bottle would be more beneficial than simply tilling in the same substance to the soil.

Sometimes the problem may be more complex and difficult to troubleshoot. In this case, a comprehensive correction may be needed. The following is a tea that is often used on plants to restore vitality.

Adding warm (not hot) water to your plants helps them to absorb the nutrients extremely quickly. Cooler water is fine for growing, since the plant takes in water at its own rate, but when "doctoring" a speedier rate is optimal. Comfrey is a healing herb that is high in calcium and phosphorus, among other things. Alfalfa is very high in nitrogen, and a good source of potassium, phosphorus and magnesium. Nettles have plant protein and stimulate the decomposition of materials in your planting soil. They are very good for the entire soil area.

There are many other teas that can be made out of a variety of ingredients. Anything that you might add to the soil or the compost pile that is rich in essential nutrients can be brewed into a tea and added to speedily deliver aid to your plants. For large plants a quart of water should suffice and for smaller plants less. Your ratio will generally be four to one. For instance, soaking one quarter of a bucket of bonemeal in one full bucket of warm water. Of this amount, one quart would be added to your plant. Remember to water your plants before adding the tea as the roots won't be able to absorb the nutrients otherwise.

Cooking With Cannabis

Most of those who cook with marijuana have found that it can be a better way to get high than smoking, as the experience tends to involve the whole body. In addition, the way in which marijuana interacts with the brain when ingested means that the high will also last longer. Medical marijuana patients, especially, find that eating is preferable to smoking, since it eliminates the need to inhale smoke, which can have a deleterious effect on their condition. Smoking, after all, is never healthy.

For a grower, eating pot makes sense on a number of different levels. In most countries, leaves and plants, even after they are harvested, are weighed and treated as if they were as potent as the bud-matter itself, and so the penalties for possession are similar. Leaves tend to be hard to dispose of, and are worthless as smokeable material. Making pot butter with leaf-matter helps growers to dispose of this material and offers a key benefit: it gets you high, with no added risk to your health.

In order to encourage budding chefs out there to make the switch to cooking with cannabis, I include a simple recipe for pot butter—a base unit for many marijuana recipes, especially cookies, cakes, and other sweet treats.

Pot Butter—the Base Unit

In order to make good butter, all you need are a large stockpot, a strainer or cheese-cloth, butter, water, and marijuana leaves. As a guide, use four ounces of leaf for every pound of butter. Making the butter is easy.

To use the butter simply substitute it for regular butter in any recipe. You can also spread it directly on toast or muffins. To store the pot butter, simply treat it as you would regular butter.

Be careful and judicious the first few times you use it, though, as the high may be truly staggering. In order to determine how strong your butter is, test it out by using half regular butter, and half pot butter. When you try it, be sure to wait at least an hour before eating more, as it takes longer for marijuana to kick in when ingested. Some factors that will vary the potency of the butter include the length of time you boiled the THC in the leaves and the strength of the leaves themselves. Be especially careful when eating the butter without cooking it in a recipe: often people will eat in one sitting what would be enough pot for a half a pan of brownies.

Once you've determined the potency of your pot butter, make your favorite desserts and enjoy! It is usually a good idea to make sweet

Cooking with Cannabis

Pot Butter—the Base Unit

1. Use four ounces of ground dried leaf or chopped fresh leaves, per pound of butter.

2. Place the butter in the stockpot and fill with enough water to cover the butter and add the leaves.

3. Simmer for at least 2½ to 3 hours, until the liquid turns green.

4. Use cheesecloth or something similar to completely strain the liquid from the leaf.

5. Let this liquid sit out to cool before storing it over-night in the refrigerator to congeal.

6. The next day, dispose of any remaining liquid. What you are left with is potent pot butter!

items because they generally call for butter and the size of a single serving is smaller. This means the body has less work to do in breaking down food before getting to the marijuana.

There are a few cookbooks out there that deal specifically with cooking and eating marijuana, including my own, *The Marijuana Chef Cookbook*. Besides the basics like cookies, fudge, and brownies, my cookbook also includes recipes for marijuana-infused drinks, like beer and martinis, as well as main courses.

Resources

Cannabis Websites

420magazine.com – cannabis growing

cannabis.com – general cannabis information

cannabisculture.com – cannabis culture news and forums

cannabishealth.com – cannabis health

canamo.net – Spanish cannabis magazine

drugpolicyfacts.org – information on drug policies

erowid.org – drug information

green-aid.com – The Medical Marijuana Legal Defense and Education Fund

grow.de – German cannabis magazine

icmag.com – Online cannabis forum

mpp.org– Marijuana Policy Project

thcene.com – German cannabis magazine

hightimes.com – *High Times* magazine

norml.org – National Organization for the Reform of Marijuana Laws

safeaccessnow.org – Americans for Safe Access

skunkmagazine.com – *Skunk Magazine*

weed.co.za – South African cannabis forum

weedworld.co.uk – British cannabis magazine information

Further Reading

Beyond Buds, Next Generation by Ed Rosenthal, Quick American Archives, September 2018

Cannabis by Robert Clarke and Mark Merlin, University of California Press, June 2016

The Cannabis Breeder's Bible by Greg Green, Green Candy Press, April, 2005

The Cannabis Encyclopedia by Jorge Cervantes, Van Patten Publishing, April 2015

The Cannabis Grow Bible by Greg Green, Green Candy Press, August 2017

Cannabis Pharmacy by Michael Backes, Black Dog & Leventhal, November, 2017

The Ganja Kitchen Revolution by Jessica Catalano, Green Candy Press, April 2023

Hemp Diseases and Pests by J.M. McPartland, R.C. Clarke, D.P. Watson, CABI Publishing, September 2000

The Marijuana Chef Cookbook by S.T. Oner, Green Candy Press, December 2022

Marijuana Garden Saver by Ed Rosenthal, Quick American Archives, May 2019

Marijuana Horticulture Fundamentals by K. of Trichome Technologies, Green Candy Press, January 2016

The Medical Cannabis Guidebook by Jeff Ditchfield and Mel Thomas, Green Candy Press, November 2014

What's Wrong with My Marijuana Plant by David Deardorff and Kathryn Wadsworth, Ten Speed Press, August 2017

Growing Supplies

advancednutrients.com

conviron.com

foxfarm.com

greenstategardener.com

growace.com

growerssupply.com

humboldtnutrients.com

hydrobuilder.com

remonutrients.com

thebucketcompany

zenhydro.com

Resources

Seedbanks and Breeders

bcbuddepot.com

brothersgrimmseeds.com

blimburnseeds.com

deliciousseeds.com

delta9labs.com

dinafem-seeds.org

truenorthseedbank.com

drgreenthumb.com

dutch-passion.nl

emeraldtriangleseeds.co.uk

evaseeds.com

lamota.org

greenhouseseeds.nl

kannabia.com

kcbrains.com

mandalaseeds.com

ministryofcannabis.com

seedsman.com

alchimiaweb.com

originalseedsstore.com

peakseedsbc.com

rainbowhouseseedco.com

riotseeds.com

ripperseeds.com

highestseeds.com

samsaraseeds.com

seedjunky.com

sonomaseeds.com

seedsman.com

seedbay.com

sensiseeds.com

somaseeds.nl

stoneygirlgardens.com

tgagenetics.com

sweetseeds.es

vulkaniaseeds.com

weedworld.co.uk

worldofseeds.eu

Index

Index

Index

genetics, and genetic variations, 15–16

marijuana, varieties of
Annunaki, 8, 16
Big Laughing, 20
Brainstorm Haze, 20
Bubba Kush, 28, 68
California Orange, 66
CH9 Flower, 86
CH9 Jack, 86
CH9 Mendocino, 86
Church, 21, 31
Colombian strains, 21
Frisian Dew, 20
Hashplant, 86
Hawaiian strains, 21
Holland's Hope, 20
Iranian Auto Flower, 89
Iranian Short Season, 32
Jack 33, 6
Jack Fem, 118
Kauai, 21
Lowryder, 19
Margoot, 113
Matanuska Tundra, 20
Maui, 21
Mexican Sativa, 20
Mexican strains, 19, 21
Niagara × Shiva, 43
NYC Diesel, 44
Romulan, 97
Sensi Star, 21
sinsemilla, 85–86
Sour Diesel, 36, 39
Southeast Asian strains, 21
Super Haze Fem, 16
medical marijuana, ix, 127

Mexican strains, characteristics of, 19, 21
mold prevention, in drying process, 104–5, 106
mulch, 37

N

nettles, in herbal tea, 123, 125
nitrogen requirements, 34, 117, 119
NORML, xiii
nutrient deficiencies, 115–21
fertilizer corrections, 125
nutrient needs
nitrogen, 34, 117, 119
phosphorous, 34, 119
potassium, 34, 119–20
soil flushing, 42
store-bought fertilizer, 34–35, 119

O

organic insecticides, 75, 121
organic soil amendments, 41–42, 120
outdoor grows
benefits of, 3–7, 4–7
camouflage materials, 43–44
disadvantages, 8–11
emergency plant fixes, 115–25
vs. indoor, 3, 3–4
local plants as guides, 42–44
overwatering, 33–34, 122, 124

P

Paradise Seeds
Sensi Star, 21
patience, 10–11
pest control, 8–9
chemical insecticides, 81
insect predators, 74–75

natural repellents, 73–81
organic insecticides, 75, 121
predator urine, 81
rodents and mammals, 77, 81
pH levels
and balanced diet, 115
and soil amendment, 41–42, 121, 125
soil testing, 37–38, 125
store-bought fertilizer, 34–35
water, 28–29, 121–22
pH test kits, 37–38, 64, 121–22
phosphorous requirements, 34, 119
in flowering stage, 41
photoperiods, manipulation of, 19
plant growth
and climate of origin, 15
leaf size, 15
soil pH, 37–38
pollination, 59–60
pot butter, 59, 127–29
potash, sulfate of, 120
potassium requirements, 34, 119–20
potency
and drying process, 102–6
THC chemistry, 16
predators, 8–9
pruning, 46
don'ts, 68–69
dos, 66
hand pruning, 67
reasons for, 65–69
training as alternative, 69
public land, 8–9, 27
pyrethrum, 75

Index

Index

troubleshooting

    emergency plant fixes, 115–25

U

underwatering, 33–34, 124–25

V

vaporizers, xii

vegetative growth stage

    blood meal, 41

W

watering requirements

    basic needs, 33–34

    chlorinated water, 125

    hand-watering, 62–63

    irrigation issues, 62–65, 122, 124

    overwatering, 33–34, 122, 124

    pH levels, 28–29, 64, 121–22

    rainwater, 29, 64–65

    underwatering, 33–34, 124–25

wind protection, 88–89

wood ashes, 42, 120

worm castings, 42, 117

Y

yields, 27

    indoor vs. outdoor grows, 3, 3–4

    predicting, 101

    and severe pruning, 68–69

    and stress, 90

Easily Grow Hundreds of Buds at Home!

With over 150 dazzling photographs by the author and easy-to-implement instructions, *Cannabis Growing Guide* is the perfect book for anyone looking to update their growing skills and get the best buds possible. Full of sage advice and charming personality, this book is what old-fashioned growers and newbies alike need to read in order to keep growing marijuana fun and fruitful.

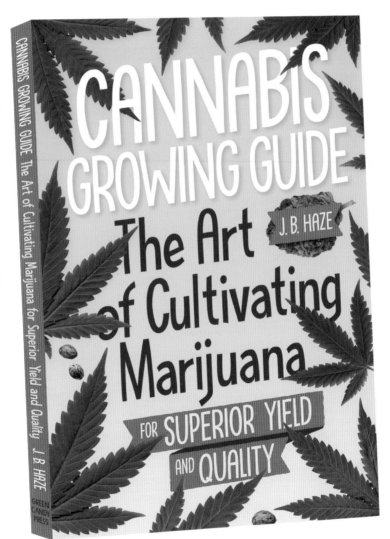

BOOKS FOR GROWING MINDS!

GREEN CANDY PRESS.com   A WHOLE NEW FLAVOR!

Join the Marijuana Edibles
Revolution!

This book will *revolutionize* the way you cook with cannabis!

The Ganja Kitchen Revolution is a unique marijuana cookbook that celebrates not just the effects of cannabis, but the myriad of unique flavors that come with it.

Chef Jessica Catalano

The Ganja Kitchen Revolution
The Bible of Cannabis Cuisine
Photography by Tyler Kittock

The Essential **Strain Specific** Guide to **MARIJUANA COOKING**

Written for all levels of skill, this book details ten different extraction methods, including oils and the infamous cannabutter, that anyone can make to enjoy these highly tasty recipes.

Brunch & Lunch! Appetizers! Drinks! Dinner! Desserts!

GREEN CANDY PRESS.COM

A WHOLE NEW FLAVOR!

Learn to Grow Your Own
HIGH-grade Bud!

Marijuana 101 offers the the perfect foundation for readers who want to become master marijuana growers.

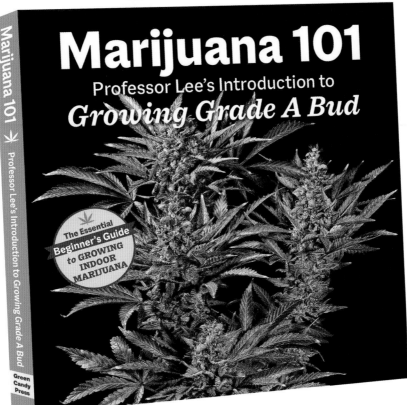

Marijuana 101

Professor Lee's Introduction to
Growing Grade A Bud

The Essential **Beginner's Guide** to GROWING INDOOR MARIJUANA

Marijuana 101 | Professor Lee's Introduction to Growing Grade A Bud

Green Candy Press

Written by Professor Lee, a highly successful grower, cultivator, and educator, *Marijuana 101* is the best introductory guide to growing great ganja and can help anyone learn how to grow their own bud.

Marijuana Outdoor Grower's Guide
The Secrets to Growing a Natural Marijuana Garden

S. T. Oner

Marijuana 101
Professor Lee's Introduction to
Growing Grade A Bud

Chef Jessica Catalano
The Ganja Kitchen Revolution
The Bible of Cannabis Cuisine
Photography by Tyler Kittock

BOOKS FOR GROWING MINDS!